THE HERITAGE OF
FRENCH
C·O·O·K·I·N·G

THE HERITAGE OF
FRENCH
C·O·O·K·I·N·G

RECIPES
THE SCOTTO SISTERS

TEXT
ANNIE HUBERT-BARE

Random House New York

Copyright © 1991 Weldon Russell Pty Ltd

Published in Australia by Weldon Russell Pty Ltd, a member of the Weldon
International Group of Companies, Sydney, and in Great Britain by Ebury
Press, an imprint of the Random Century Group Pty Ltd, London.

Publisher: Elaine Russell
Managing editor: Dawn Titmus
Editor: Ariana Klepac
Translators: Marlyse Lupis, Barbara McGilvray, Barbara Santich
Copy-editors: Beverley Barnes, Jill Wayment
Picture researcher: CLAM!
US cooking consultant: Mardee Haidin Regan
Design concept: Susan Kinealy
Designer: Catherine Martin
Food photographers: Jon Bader, Rowan Fotheringham
Food stylists: Marie Hélène Clauzon, Carolyn Fienberg
Caption writer: Lynn Humphries
Indexer: Dianne Regtop
Production: Jane Hazell

Library of Congress Cataloging-in-Publication Data

Scotto. E. (Elisabeth)
  The heritage of French cooking / by Elisabeth Scotto. Marianne Comolli,
  and Annie Hubert-Baré.
  256 p. 33.5 x 24.5 cm.
  ISBN 0-679-40478-3
  1. Cookery, French. 2. Cookery — France. I. Comolli, Marianne. II.
  Hubert-Baré, Annie. III. Title.
  TX719.S389 1991 641.5944—dc20 91–10430

Produced by Weldon Russell Pty Ltd
4/52 Ourimbah Road
Mosman NSW 2088 Australia

Typeset by Savage Type Pty Ltd, Brisbane, Australia
Colour separation by Scantrans, Singapore
Produced by Mandarin Offset, Hong Kong

A KEVIN WELDON PRODUCTION

Manufactured in Hong Kong
24689753
First American Edition

Front cover: *The pavements of Les Halles*, Victor Gilbert
(1847–1933); MUSEE DES BEAUX-ARTS, LE HAVRE

Back cover: *The kinds of liberality*, illustration from *Ethics,
Politics and Economics* by Aristotle (French manuscript
1452–57); BIBLIOTHEQUE MUNICIPALE, ROUEN

Endpapers: *Basket of peaches*, Pierre Dupuis (1610–82);
PRIVATE COLLECTION

Opp. title page: *Bowl of fruit and flowers*, François Bonvin
(1817–87); MUSEE DES BEAUX ARTS, LILLE

Title page: *The bar at the Folies-Bergères*, Edouard Manet
(1832–83); COURTAULD INSTITUTE GALLERIES, LONDON

Still life with basket, Paul Cézanne (1836–1906); MUSEE D'ORSAY, PARIS

CONTENTS

The meal, François Boucher (1703–70); THE LOUVRE, PARIS

The boating-party luncheon (detail), Pierre Auguste Renoir (1841–1919); PHILLIPS COLLECTION, WASHINGTON, DC The theme of people relaxing outdoors, untrammeled by the deman

...work, was one to which the Impressionists frequently returned.

INTRODUCTION

The French, more than any other nationality, have refined the art of eating into a model of subtlety, variety, and elegance. French cuisine has influenced every Western cuisine, to the extent that it has become an international symbol of prestige and quality. Where else in the world does the table become the center of impassioned talk on the subject of eating? If we were Japanese some of our cooks would be declared "living national treasures." As it is, we are happy to award them the medal of the Legion of Honor and turn them into stars.

This grand culinary tradition, many centuries old, is an integral part of our culture. But by what route did France become the cradle of gastronomy? Certainly, this magnificent country is blessed with one of the most temperate of climates and an extraordinary abundance and diversity of produce from its different regions.

But the existence of one of the world's greatest gastronomies cannot be explained simply by the presence of fine produce; it needs its practitioners. Many people through the centuries have helped effect a slow transformation, and forged the characteristics of a tradition of fine cooking and eating that continues to evolve today.

Just how far back should we go to find the start of gastronomic activities in this land? Without doubt, back to the time when two very different populations, the Gauls and the Romans, confronted one another, then intermixed. According to Latin sources the Gauls were coarse eaters and great beer-drinkers, who excelled in raising pigs from which they made superb hams. The colonizing Romans brought two essentials: the vine with its wine, and olive oil. They encouraged the Gauls to grow wheat instead of barley and rye, and brought with them prized ingredients such as "garum," made from the brine of salted and fermented fish; the strong, garlic-flavored asafoetida; and the pepper and the cinnamon that came to be used just as much in Gallo-Roman territories as in Rome itself.

In the dark period of the great invasions after the fall of the Roman Empire, the Gallo-Roman traditions fused with contributions from the barbarian invaders, whether Franks, or Goths, or Vandals, and were gradually transformed into what we now call medieval cuisine. From the fifth to the tenth century, in the royal and ecclesiastical courts where an abundance of produce and resources was available, the characteristics of a culinary art were developed.

The breakfast room, Pierre Bonnard (1867–1947); THE MUSEUM OF MODERN ART, NEW YORK
Bonnard's propensity for depicting serene interiors and family scenes around a table set with a simple repast — and the technique he employed in painting them — became known as *Intimisme*. In the latter part of his career his pictures, such as this one painted *circa* 1930, became increasingly colorful and filled with light.

As dining in a recumbent position fell from favor and sitting upright to eat became the norm, dishes based on finely chopped ingredients were displaced by large joints of beef, pork, poultry, and game. Carving became an art, and was a task entrusted to the carving officer who held an important position in the blossoming hierarchy of noble households. Meat was synonymous with status, and was to retain its symbolic significance until the latter half of the twentieth century. The range of spices and seasonings changed: garum and asafoetida, for example, disappeared completely, while cloves and nutmegs entered the repertoire.

CUISINE IN THE MEDIEVAL ERA

The first French culinary texts left to us, dating from about 1300, are treatises intended for the privileged classes; there is scant record of what the poor and the peasants ate. The aristocrats received produce from their lands as tributes, and they claimed exclusive hunting rights. The townspeople had access to supplies from the market gardeners and farmers on the edge of the towns, while the monasteries were self-sufficient, amply provisioned by their own holdings.

The supply of food depended on seasonal variations and the Church calendar, which determined days of meat-eating and days of "fasting." In France at this time, Christians "fasted" on average one day in three! "Fasting" meant abstaining from all products of land animals, eggs and milk included, which were believed to "kindle lust and passion." There were often two versions of the same recipe, one for "fast" days, the other for meat-eating days or *jours gras*; in the former, meat was replaced by fish, milk by almond milk, meat stock by fish stock or wine or sometimes the liquid drained from cooked dried peas.

Bread oven, Gallo-Roman mosaic (third century);
MUSEE DES ANTIQUITES NATIONALES, SAINT-GERMAIN-EN-LAYE
Bread has long held an important place in the French diet. Flat cakes of millet, oats, barley, and occasionally wheat were baked in Ancient Gaul. The Romans favored wheat and often flavored their breads with poppy, fennel, or cumin seeds.

Servants roasting poultry, tapestry by Queen Mathilde (*circa* 1080);
MUSEE DE L'EVECHE, BAYEUX
The poultry is being threaded on to skewers before being cooked over an open fire or glowing coals.

To ensure provisions in lean times, fattened pigs, cattle, and sheep were slaughtered at the start of winter and their meat variously salted and smoked. The fat was stored in large pots. Salt was used to preserve green vegetables, mushrooms were dried and fruits were cooked in honey.

None of the products of the Americas had yet made an appearance. Tomatoes, bell peppers (capsicums), potatoes, pumpkins, beans, turkey, chocolate, and coffee were unknown. Sugar and rice were part of the pharmacopoeia; considered food for invalids, they were only slowly accepted into French cuisine.

Bread was the staple found on every table. The three basic variations in texture accorded with the main rungs of the social ladder: fine for the wealthy; coarser for the merchants and town craftspeople; solid and heavy for the peasants and workers. Whether in the courts or the towns, bread was made by specialist bakers. In the country peasants were obliged to take their bread to be baked in the ovens belonging to their lords.

These were carnivorous centuries. Meat was the supreme ingredient — if not in practice, at least in spirit. In the towns the corporation of butchers enjoyed great influence.

Shopping in a covered arcade in France, illumination from a manuscript of Aristotle's *Ethics, politics and economics* (fifteenth century);
BIBLIOTHEQUE MUNICIPALE, ROUEN
Aristotle (d. 322 BC) wrote extensively on every branch of science and philosophy known in his day, and made many observations on the science of food. His work was rediscovered in the Middle Ages and continued to be of influence throughout the Renaissance. He combined close observation with acute reasoning; therein lay his appeal for the Renaissance mind.

Reflections of history, Vincent de Beauvais (fifteenth-century manuscript);
MUSEE CONDE, CHANTILLY
The monastic orders lived off their lands and produced their own bread, wine, and cheeses. To a large degree, their cooking shaped regional gastronomy.

Naturally the quality of the animals sent to market varied, but the fact that freshly slaughtered meat was sold every day puts paid to the myth that medieval cuisine was highly spiced to mask rancidity. Pork, veal, and lamb were considered suitable for the "delicate" digestive systems of the aristocracy.

The nobility also laid claim to pheasants, peacocks, fat hens, swans, and other species of feathered exotica that they regarded as central to their elaborate festive banquets. There was a passion for decorating or camouflaging such foodstuffs. Swans and peacocks, for example, were roasted and re-covered with their plumage for serving, their beaks and feet embellished with gold leaf. This habit was to reach its peak in the nineteenth century with the architectural presentations of Carême.

Milk was difficult to keep fresh and played little part in the daily diet. Brie and Roquefort were already famous and they, along with other cheeses, were either served in their plain state or used as ingredients in various dishes and pastries. Eggs were an essential except, of course, on "fast" days.

Fish was consumed year round by the fortunate wealthy who stocked their own rivers and ponds. For those living inland, fresh seafood was a rarity: it was transported along the River Seine as far as Paris, but what condition was it in when it arrived? Salted cod and herring were omnipresent on "fast"-day tables. Whale was included in the same category as fish and was widely eaten. Like pork, the meat was salted, and the fat was used by the poorer classes in cooking.

Doctors considered that vegetables lacked nourishment compared to bread or meat. Leafy and root vegetables, served as thick purées, were relegated to the kitchens of the poor, although they were not entirely overlooked by the more thrifty and prudent of the bourgeois. Fruit and nuts, on the other hand, did have a place on the tables of the wealthy.

There is evidence of a predilection for strongly flavored but not excessive combinations of spices and herbs. Pepper became popular, but cooks to the aristocracy spurned it in favor of the more expensive *menues épices* (small spices) — cloves, nutmeg, mace, grain of paradise (*Aframomum meleguetta*). In addition, they used galingale, long pepper, cinnamon, ginger, cardamom, caraway, and hyssop.

In the nineteenth century the bourgeois was to denounce medieval cuisine as composed of "abominable stews." In fact, it was a "light" cuisine — not as one might apply the word to describe Nouvelle Cuisine, for example, but in the sense that it made little use of fats. Oil, butter, cream, pork fat, and flour were absent from the sauces. Instead, cooks used vinegar, wine, or verjuice (the juice of very acidic or unripe grapes) and occasionally the juice of lemons, bitter oranges, or pomegranates. Carefully ground spices were then added. The flavor most savored was sour-spicy, sometimes with a hint of bitterness. Sugar was seldom added; the salty-sweet combination was, and has remained, the preserve of other European cuisines.

Visual effect was of prime importance, and recipes stressed the color to be used. Green hues were obtained from the leaves of leeks or from spinach juice; saffron, very frequently used and the most costly of spices, yielded yellow. Sunflowers or sandalwood produced shades of red; and all kinds of substances, including milk or almond milk, were used in white dishes.

This was the golden age of pies — gigantic creations that contained whole roast birds, fish, or pieces of meat. The pastry had none of the lightness achieved in later centuries

The life of famous women: The wife of Mithridate, Ipsicrethea, at table, Antoine du Four (early sixteenth century);
MUSEE DOBREE, NANTES

and served more as a sturdy pot encasing the ingredients as they cooked. Sweet dishes included waffles, *talmouses* (little cakes which are still made today), fritters, tarts made with milk or cheese, and fresh fruits.

The great vineyard areas of France were already established and wine was commonly drunk, sometimes diluted with water, and used in cooking. At the close of meals, hippocras (mulled wine with sugar and spices) was served heated, spiced and sweetened. Beer, cider, and perry made from pears were also available.

Around 1326 the man who was to become the first great French cook to leave his mark on the history of gastronomy came on the scene. Guillaume Tirel from Normandy was a young lad when he became kitchen hand for Jeanne d'Èvreux, wife of King Charles IV. His apprenticeship was long and harsh and everything was learnt in the oral tradition. He became a *potagier* specializing in long-simmered dishes, and gradually rose through the culinary ranks. His fellow cooks nicknamed him "Taillevent" apparently in reference to his speed and dexterity. In 1346 he became master cook to King Philippe VI, and subsequently, under Charles VI, he reached the pinnacle — *écuyer de cuisine* (kitchen steward) and *maître des garnisons du roi* (master of the king's garrison). His illustrious career lasted sixty years, in the service of five kings.

The hunt, P. de Crescens (fifteenth century); MUSEE CONDE, CHANTILLY
This illustration from the illuminated manuscript *Rustican* depicts the slaying of game and plundering of nests. The nobility enjoyed sole hunting rights, until such privileges were abolished, but this did not deter poachers. The wild boar (known in French hunting terms as *bête noire* — black beast) was hotly pursued; the flesh of the young animals is delicate but its taste becomes very pronounced as the animal reaches adulthood.

It should be noted that in royal households the master cook or *chef cuisinier* commanded great respect. Not so the female cooks generally employed by the bourgeois — their standing was considerably lower on the culinary scale even though their contribution to French gastronomy has often been of great significance. For many centuries the culinary arts were peremptorily decreed a male preserve, a situation which largely is still true today.

Taillevent compiled a book, *Le Viandier de Taillevent*, which comprised recipes from two anonymous manuscripts (the remains of which still exist), and others of his own invention. He drew on the oldest collection of recipes in the French language yet known to us, named *Petit traité de 1306*, and the Sion manuscript, dated 1326, and his own expertise to produce a book that was to remain a bestseller until the seventeenth century and was published regularly up to the beginning of the eighteenth century.

The most lively collection of recipes of the medieval period was not the work of a cook but of an unknown elderly Parisian bourgeois who, in about 1390, decided to write a treatise of moral and domestic economy for his very young wife. He borrowed recipes from the *Viandier* and added his comments, together with other more ordinary recipes which made full use of "vulgar" vegetables and the typical provisions. He also left us menus for all kinds of occasions, together with advice on household management and glimpses of techniques that were common in kitchens at the time.

Medieval France perfected the art of the banquet, a theatrical meal rich in ritual, which offered the opportunity to affirm one's rank, wealth, and prestige. This tradition has been upheld in French culture — at every grand national, family, or social celebration.

The banquets took place in a room practically bare of furniture save for an imposing sideboard on which all the luxury items of the household and the wine were placed. The dining-table was made from planks set on trestles and guests were seated along one side of it to make service easier, but also so that the *entremets* — performances by actors, jugglers and musicians — could be best appreciated. All guests had a thick slice of bread, the "trencher," placed in front of them to be used as a plate. Liquid preparations were served in shallow bowls, one for every two guests. Thus a meal described as "ten bowls" indicated twenty guests. Spoons, knives, and napkins were used, but forks had yet to appear.

There might be six or more *mets*, each comprising ten or so dishes, and guests served themselves from the dish in front of them. This was the beginning of what was known as *service à la française*, where all the dishes were set on the table in a series of groups (almost as though, in today's terms, you went to a restaurant and were served the whole menu). This system persisted until the mid-nineteenth century when it was replaced by the still-practised *service à la russe*.

The banquet, with its numerous lavish dishes, was impressive. Compared to today's modest offerings, so too were the meals comprising three main *mets* (dishes) that were served in respectable bourgeois households. But it must be remembered that the host's social standing demanded such a display of generosity; the meals should be thought of as similar to today's Chinese banquets where guests eat only a little of what they want or what they find in front of them. Heavy eaters our ancestors may have been, but nobody ate everything.

Although denigrated for centuries, certain elements of medieval cuisine were instrumental in effecting some changes in the sixteenth and seventeenth centuries. These in turn made possible the creation of important precepts of classical cuisine.

THE RENAISSANCE

In the fields of science and the arts, the Renaissance in France witnessed significant advances. The same cannot be said of cuisine, for it seemed that taste and techniques had stagnated both in the kitchen and at the table. Yet other forces were at work that would bring about change during the following century.

The only reference books for the culinary arts remained the medieval works, with *Le Viandier* still the great classic. But now cuisine became the focus of literary endeavor, a situation that has flourished ever since. The source of this interest in writing about food was the new attitude to the body and to health put forward by the doctors. Their discourses on dietary rules greatly influenced intellectuals and scholars. Compositions ranged from the writings of Montaigne on his food preferences, to snippets of Rabelaisian bravura detailing the homeric appetites of Pantagruel . . . and a little later, the poet Ronsard devoted a sonnet to the salad.

Feast of the nobility, School of Fontainebleau (sixteenth century); MUSÉE GRANET, AIX-EN-PROVENCE
There were two Schools of Fontainebleau, the first starting with the patronage of François I, the second enjoying that of Henry IV in the latter half of the sixteenth century. Italian artists such as Primaticcio and Rosso introduced the Mannerist-influenced style into the French royal palaces. Typically, figures are painted in elegant, somewhat strained if not extreme poses — often *contrapposto* (contraposed).

The tasting, in the style of Abraham Bosse (*circa* 1635); MUSEE DES BEAUX-ARTS, TOURS Catherine de' Medici is credited with introducing the artichoke to France from her native Tuscany. Her fondness for the vegetable was considered scandalous because it was reputed to be an aphrodisiac and not something a young woman (Catherine was 14 when she married Henry II) should be seen to eat.

New ingredients from the New World, such as chocolate and potatoes, and coffee from the Middle East, began to provoke interest. Also, following the long wars between France and Italy, the diplomatic exchanges and royal marriages, fruits and vegetables from the Italian peninsula made their way into French kitchens — artichokes, different varieties of melon, peas, and salad greens. Sugar, once used for its therapeutic properties, became increasingly available. The astrologer and alchemist Michel de Nostre-Dame, known as Nostradamus, wrote one of the first French works on confectionery, in which he included recipes for jams and preserved fruits. However, his compatriots remained faithful to the medieval taste for the spicy or the sour and continued, unlike the Italians, to limit their sugar consumption in cooking.

Italian fashions also became evident in tableware: forks made an appearance, and it was now considered bad manners to pick up morsels of food in one's fingers. Individual plates ousted the "trencher," and crockery and glass were used instead of pewter. Kitchen equipment underwent slight modifications, the main one being the introduction of a small, secondary hearth which functioned as a cooking range alongside the traditional open fireplace with its broilers (grills) and spits.

Finally, the meal became more sophisticated and included a greater diversity of dishes. The three principal courses, or *services* as they were now known, remained the same as in the medieval period. At a banquet, for example, the first course or *entrée de table* would feature hot, generally liquid dishes such as *potages*, *fricassées*, and hashes. The second included roast and boiled meats, and poultry. Hippocras, dried fruits, wafers, and little cakes might be served for dessert. Finally, the *issue de table*, served in a separate room, featured cold dishes such as fruits, dairy foods, and sweet items.

The shift towards the establishment of a new "classic" cuisine was slowly taking place, but the first written evidence of this was not seen until the seventeenth century.

THE BIRTH OF THE *GRANDE CUISINE*

Grande cuisine was established in France during the seventeenth and eighteenth centuries and became an international symbol of good taste. It reigned supreme in wealthy households, in luxury hotels, and on ocean vessels. While it demanded the skills of highly trained professionals, in more modest households *cuisine bourgeoise* and "regional cuisine" were being shaped by nonprofessional cooks, often women.

Picnic at the court of Burgundy, copy of a lost Flemish original by the School of Van Eyck (sixteenth century); CHATEAU DE VERSAILLES
The meal, following a falconry expedition, took place on the eve of Philip the Good's marriage to Duchess Isabella of Portugal in 1430. *Chasse,* the French term for the hunt which had just taken place, was also the name of a meat course consisting entirely of roast game presented on an enormous platter.

Madame la marquise de Lude, engraving by Pierre Bonnart (seventeenth century); CHATEAU DE VERSAILLES
The marquise and her companion are savoring several little morsels, among them a flat biscuit — *oublie* — which was the ancestor of the waffle. *Oublies* were particularly popular during the Middle Ages, though their history dates back further than that. Their name may come from the Greek *obelios* (a cake cooked between two iron plates and sold for an *obol*) or from the Latin *oblata* (offering).

In the seventeenth century, the popularity of spices waned dramatically in France, all the more surprising as it had been Europe's major consumer. Saffron was detested, and only pepper, cloves, and nutmeg, in barely discernible quantities, remained acceptable. Aromatic herbs fell out of favor also. Hyssop, rue, and marjoram were replaced by thyme, bay leaf, parsley, savory, chives, tarragon, and rosemary, all of which have retained their popularity to the present day. The strict differentiation made by the French between the salty and sweet was finally established in this era.

Vegetable dishes containing pumpkins, lentils, root vegetables, chicory, and asparagus had only recently been considered peasant fare. At best, they were a novelty. Now they began to gain acceptance by the aristocracy. Morels and truffles (the latter in particular) disappeared from the tables of the common people to grace virtually exclusively those of the wealthy. Such an extraordinary reversal of values was possibly a response to the renewed search for "nature," and to society's eternal quest for the Holy Grail.

Ingredients such as anchovies and capers from the South of France infiltrated various recipes. It seemed that *grande cuisine* was shedding many of its previous characteristics and was drawing inspiration from the ordinary essentials of bourgeois and peasant kitchens.

At last we see the triumph of butter, now allowed during Lent and on "fast" days. Like truffles, it quickly became a fundamental in classic cuisine, although cream remained largely overlooked. In addition to butter, there was now a significant increase in the use of pork fat, lard, and oils, primarily in sauces.

The flour-and-butter *roux* was born and proved indispensable as a thickening agent. It is first mentioned in *Le Cuisinier François*, the bestseller of the seventeenth century and the first book in which set rules and principles of food preparation were laid down. It was written in 1651 by François de La Varenne, *écuyer de cuisine* (kitchen steward) to the Marquis d'Uxelles. It also featured in *L'Art de Bien Traiter* compiled several years later by an author violently opposed to La Varenne and known only by the initials L.S.R.

Other important innovations included the technique of reduction which gave sauces a good consistency and provided a base for a variety of dishes. *Jus* or gravy was the result of deglazing the pans in which meats had roasted, and *coulis* or *cullis* was based on concentrated meat stock perfumed with herbs and thickened with bread. These were the ancestors of the *fonds de cuisine*, the basic preparations on which nineteenth-century cooks would construct a whole theory of cooking. François Massialot, the last of the great cooks of the seventeenth century, gives no fewer than twenty-three recipes for the preparation of *cullis*. The era of sauces had begun.

And this was not all! Cooks were starting to make mousses, the preparation of which was immensely complicated — today, we can rely on food processors to do the hard work. Mousses made from meat and fish represented the peak of sophistication and were intended especially for the ladies. They were given names such as *godiveau, quenelle*, and *boudin* and today we find them in the form of the *boudin blanc* or in the classic *quenelles* which are masterpieces of the cuisine of Lyons.

While the aristocracy set itself apart by establishing rules of "good taste" in its kitchens, the bourgeoisie, treading in its footsteps, became a significant market for the new cookbooks. Nicolas de Bonnefons, valet to the young King Louis XIV, was the author of two volumes: *Le Jardinier François*, and *Les Délices de la Campagne*, published in 1654.

The hunt lunch, François Lemoyne (1688–1737); MUSEUM OF ART, SAO PAULO Known mainly as a history painter, Lemoyne won the coveted commission to decorate the ceiling of the Salon d'Hercule in Versailles. He completed the work *The apotheosis of Hercules* for Louis XV in 1736, and committed suicide the following year.

These books were intended for country squires and the landed gentry, as well as members of the new bourgeoisie who invested in country estates. The first volume is concerned principally with horticulture and the preservation of foods; the second addresses the subject of cuisine. Bonnefons was a passionate "modernist," and one of his basic principles was that ingredients should retain the flavors with which nature endowed them.

These recipes are more simple, and usually less costly, than those found in the works of L.S.R. or La Varenne. They illustrate a kind of *cuisine bourgeoise* which continued to evolve up to the twentieth century, in the wake of important trends in the aristocratic and professional cuisine. Another new feature is that the author addresses "ladies" and a particular type of "lady" who wouldn't hesitate to investigate what goes on in the kitchen and, if necessary, lend a hand.

Despite disagreement from those who held fast to tradition, the taste for natural flavors in cooking, the improvement in the quality of fruits and vegetables, and the reappraisal of a *cuisine bourgeoise* based on regional produce from one's own country signified that the scene was set for the Enlightened Century.

The cup of chocolate (The Duc de Penthièvre and his family),
J. B. Charpentier (painted *circa* 1767–68);
MUSEE DE L'ABBAYE, FONTAINE-CHAALIS
Cortez learned from the Aztecs how to turn the cacao bean into a drink and a paste — the forerunner of the chocolate bar. The Spanish endeavored to keep the secret to themselves but it reached France when Jews expelled from Spain began processing chocolate in the Bayonne region. The product was viewed with suspicion until Anne of Austria (who was Spanish) married Louis XIII in 1615; she made chocolate a drink of the French court.

THE EIGHTEENTH CENTURY

In this eventful century which culminated in revolution, the style of serving ceremonial meals slowly changed. Towards the end of the seventeenth century and until the death of Louis XIV in 1715, table ceremony reached the zenith of formality. Once or twice a week at Versailles, the spectacle of the king dining was there for all to see, and it was played like a true theatrical piece, with the maître d'hôtel as the stage manager. But with the new century and the accession of Philippe d'Orléans, the Regent, some important changes were instigated.

The Regent was a man who liked to eat well. He equated "good taste" with intimacy and conviviality and introduced the fashion for suppers with only a few guests and a minimum of servants in attendance. In some establishments the table disappeared through a trapdoor between courses, reappearing as if by magic, loaded with the next course. Thus political discussions and romantic liaisons could be conducted virtually unimpeded. It was hardly surprising that foodstuffs such as raw oysters, eggwhites, certain broths and *ragoûts* were consumed as much for their supposed powers as aphrodisiacs as for their culinary worth.

The Ancients and Moderns waged a war of words in the grand kitchens, continuing the battle that had commenced the previous century. The Moderns envisaged a future in which simplicity and "natural" purity reigned. This trend was well established by the 1740s but, in reality, there was nothing simple about this *cuisine nouvelle*. It was labor intensive, extravagant, and complicated, featuring flavors of enormous complexity.

There was much theorizing, of course. François Marin, author of *Les Dons de Comus, ou Les Délices de la Table*, wrote in 1739: "Modern cuisine is a kind of chemistry." In *La Science du Maître d'Hôtel Cuisinier*, Menon, another author of several culinary treatises, had earlier remarked: "Cookery refines the coarse elements of foodstuffs, strips the tiniest pieces to take advantage of the earthy extracts they contain. It brings them to perfection, purifies them and, in a way, transforms them."

This is the language of alchemy and, indeed, there is a parallel between the chemists in their search for a quintessence and the cooks in their pursuit of the perfect sauce. The era of a technique based on elemental mixtures that could be adapted to all circumstances was underway.

Marin was one of the greatest cooks of the century and elevated sauces into a class of their own; his creations were close relatives of the creamy *velouté* sauces dear to the following century.

Menon was among the best known and most widely read authors of his day. His *Souper de la Cour* gave theoretical and technical advice to professional cooks while *Cuisinière Bourgeoise*, the new bestseller, was a commonsense work addressed to women, with recipes based on the produce of garden and market. Another fine cook, Vincent de la Chapelle, compiled *Le Cuisinier Moderne* in which, like Marin, he set down the fundamental principles of *grande cuisine*; his *sauce espagnole* (Spanish sauce) is still a classic.

As modern scientific theories were advanced, philosophy flourished, and the Revolution began to simmer, cuisine followed its own path. Grand households continued to

The jar of olives, Jean Baptiste Siméon Chardin (1699–1779); THE LOUVRE, PARIS

A fine supper, J. M. Moreau (1741–1814);
PRIVATE COLLECTION
This engraving (dated 1781) shows a small group of merry people enjoying each other's company just as much as the food. The fashion for intimate suppers was established by the regent.

spend lavishly on eating and drinking. For the bourgeois, whose means limited the extent to which aristocratic trends could be copied, cuisine became a compromise. There were fewer and less complicated dishes and greater advantage was taken of regional specialties. The enlightened members of the aristocracy paid some heed to *cuisine bourgeoise*, sometimes for reasons of health, sometimes through a concern for equality.

Books such as *La Maison Rustique* spread the principles of *cuisine bourgeoise* to provincial families; like all culinary styles of the period, it had developed in the kitchens of the capital. And for good reason — Paris was better supplied. For the great cooks the capital was the only place to work.

New and "unusual" foods now became commonplace. The first Parisian cafés had been established, and served as venues for passionate political debate. Tea, coffee, and chocolate had become everyday beverages. Ice-cream, once the preserve of nobility, was served at one café. Procope, and green beans, pumpkin, and potato made their debuts. *Pâté de foie gras* (goose-liver pâté) was a specialty of the Alsace region that became extremely popular. And in Normandy a certain Marie Harel, in her village of Camembert, made a cheese that would be prized worldwide.

Since the medieval period there had been inns and taverns for the working classes, where drink and a limited fixed menu (*table d'hôte*) were served. Because of the restrictions imposed by the guilds concerned with the preparation of food, some establishments could sell ragoûts but not roasts; others could sell broths but not pies; and so on.

There were no restaurants as we know them today. The word "restaurant" originally meant a restorative or broth, and came to mean an eating house only in 1765 when a certain Boulanger opened a small establishment where he served such *restaurants* to his clients. He laid the food out on small marble tables and inspired other "restaurateurs" to set up shop in a similar manner. However, the first real restaurants, temples to the *grande cuisine française*, were not established until the latter years of the Revolution.

Only with the first stirrings of the Revolution was the guilds' grip released and monopolies and privileges abolished. A "restaurateur" was now authorized to serve meals that included all categories of dishes. In 1789, a prophetic date, Antoine de Beauvilliers opened a restaurant in Paris that became an instant success. It was much favored by the aristocracy, a fact that cost Beauvilliers ten months of imprisonment during the Terror. But on his release he simply opened another in the Palais Royal area which became a showplace of gastronomy.

Restaurants multiplied as aristocrats fled and their cooks had to find other jobs. The era of great restaurants had now begun, with some restaurateurs becoming national celebrities. At the Frères Provençaux, Mediterranean specialties such as *bouillabaisse* (fish stews or soup) and *brandade de morue* (salt cod, potato, and garlic purée) put in their first appearance, and tomatoes, until then absent from the *grande cuisine*, were featured.

The leaders of the Revolution were often gourmands: Mirabeau, Danton, Saint-Just and the others enjoyed homeric dinners in restaurants such as Méot and the Frères Provençaux. Even those who were condemned took pleasure in their food: restaurateurs had contracts with well-to-do prisoners and presented them with exquisite meals before they went off to the guillotine.

Haute cuisine descended to street level, the best chefs had restaurants, and every citizen with money to spend could eat as well as any of the "late" nobles.

THE NINETEENTH-CENTURY GOURMANDS

Under the Directory (the executive of France from 1795 to 1799), and until the beginning of the First Empire in 1804, by which time the horrors of the Terror had finally receded, the French plunged into a frenzy of gourmandism and indulgence. The country began to live again.

Gourmands picked up their pens and wrote about the pleasures of eating in a way that was scholarly, serious, and almost religious. Grimod de La Reynière was the first to publish a gastronomic magazine. This son of a tax-collector, who had formally cut himself off from his family, was handicapped by a genetic malformation of the hands. He seems to have compensated for his drawbacks with his passion for food. Women ran a poor second judging by his comment, "What woman, however pretty she may be, can compete with the superb partridges from the Languedoc and the Cevennes . . ."

Parisian storekeepers lined up to offer La Reynière their best products, to be tasted and reviewed in his *Almanach des Gourmands*.

The fairground at Quimper, O. Perrin (1761–1832);
MUSEE DES BEAUX-ARTS, QUIMPER
The country fair depicted here (painted in 1810) was just one of the many to which people came to buy goods and enjoy themselves. The great annual fairs were held on the parish's saint's day. Some were the forerunners of important agricultural shows still held today, some specialized in a limited range of produce while others were more diverse.

La Physiologie du Goût, a landmark in gastronomic literature, was written by another sophisticated gourmet and man-of-the-world, Jean-Anthelme Brillat-Savarin. It is an impassioned series of reflections on gastronomy, and while offering few recipes, is packed with anecdotes and recollections of simple and formal meals.

The intimate suppers of the eighteenth century and their delicate scenes of seduction now gave way to meals concerned only with the pleasures of the palate. No sexual intrigues here. These dinners were often men-only affairs, not to say misanthropic — the gourmand would go alone to a well-reputed restaurant.

At the other end of the spectrum, in a century filled with political and diplomatic events, the *grande cuisine* graced the splendid mansions of those who were rebuilding France. The chef for these generals and strategists, among them Talleyrand, was Antonin Carême, the master of the decorative and the edible. Only he could have conjured food of suitable magnificence for a function held in 1816 to honor the National Guard, at which more than 3,000 guests were present.

Although Paris did not produce any raw ingredients, the best products from the four corners of the world converged there. According to Grimod de La Reynière, "It is the place

A corner of the vineyard, Languedoc 1886,
Edouard Debat-Ponson (1847–1913);
MUSEE DES BEAUX-ARTS, NANTES
Among Languedoc's top vintages today are Tavel rosé and Limoux sparkling white.

Country meal (detail), Auguste B. Glaize (1807–93); MUSEE FABRE, MONTPELLIER
Informal gatherings at meals in the open air became an increasingly popular subject among artists in the late nineteenth century.

where the respective qualities of everything that man uses for food are best appreciated and where the ways of transforming them for the benefit of our senses are best understood." France, in this period, considered itself the beacon of culture for all civilized societies and the center of the world. Paris, therefore, was the world capital of cuisine and good taste.

During this century, which has been qualified (perhaps somewhat too arbitrarily) as "the golden age of French gastronomy," the fundamental principles of culinary technique which were to be the model for international gastronomy were formulated. From the ovens of the great cooks emerged dishes that would become international classics. But what were conditions like for these artists? The kitchen range, eventually of cast iron, was introduced and was gradually modified and improved. With this modern miracle, cooks could perform almost any culinary operation, and the enormous fireplace with its spits lost its central role. Grand kitchens were superbly organized, with a veritable army of specialists and kitchen hands, all under the rod of the head "chef." The different techniques and all the important fundamental preparations were codified and, arranged according to category, were always on hand for dishes as luxurious as they were varied.

Lunch, Claude Monet (1840–1926);
Monet painted many pictures of his
favorite model, Camille Doncieux (whom
he married in 1870), and their son, Jean.
He imbued simple, everyday occurrences
with great warmth and charm.

Two "new" techniques were perfected, both involving long, slow cooking of meat or
poultry in covered pots: the *poêlé* or pot-roast, and the *braisé* (braised dishes). They bore
certain similarities to the *estouffades* of the Middle Ages and the *ragoûts* of the
Renaissance. Now, taking the *fonds* or gravies as their foundation, they were codified and
included in the culinary repertoire.

Paradoxically, the most important inventions were entirely overlooked. Preservation
by sterilization, discovered by Nicholas Appert, and refrigeration, pioneered by Ferdinand
Carré and Charles Tellier, remained in the wings until the early twentieth century.

The quest for fixed values and stability was characteristic of bourgeois society, and it made its mark on food. The airy mousses of the previous century were reworked and became dense *farces* or forcemeats that were only one element in a more complicated dish. Food was encased in aspic and sauces became thicker and all-enveloping, masking what lay beneath. The use of butter and fats increased and rounded out the flavors of the dishes as well as their consumers.

Another fundamental change came in the manner in which meals were served. *Service à la française*, whereby all the dishes in a particular course were set out at the one time from which the guests would choose, began to wane in the early nineteenth century. It survived longest in bourgeois households where hosts regarded it as a potent symbol of their wealth and success.

Service à la russe now predominated. The various dishes were served one after the other, presented directly to the guest. The food, carved and arranged in the kitchen, could be served hot. Though not as esthetically pleasing as its predecessor, *service à la russe* was more practical and egalitarian, and showed the cook's efforts off to best advantage.

Now how would the affluent flaunt their wealth? By revitalizing a striking feature of medieval banquets — the *grosses pièces*. These were extraordinary, enormous arrangements of foodstuffs which, although edible, were constructed more with the impact of their appearance in mind. On sideboards and tables there appeared extravagant pieces made from sugar, marzipan, lard, and any other malleable ingredient. The luminary Antonin

Tea in the garden, Louis Carré (early twentieth century);
MUSEE D'ORSAY, PARIS

Lunch in the conservatory, Louise Abbema (1858–1927); MUSEE DES BEAUX-ARTS, PAU

Saucepan and egg, G. Rohner (b. 1913);
PRIVATE COLLECTION

Carême, whose edible edifices included the Great Ruins of Athens and the Great Fountain of Parnassus, set the tone when he wrote that pastry-making was the finest branch of architecture. Not surprisingly, his contemporaries compared him to that sixteenth-century giant of Italian architecture, Palladio.

Carême left behind a considerable volume of written work on the rules and theory of classical cuisine. Thanks to him and celebrated disciples such as Urbain Dubois, Jules Gouffé, Duglére and Escoffier, the French system was accepted as the international model. As tourism opened up and high society "took the waters," traveled to the beauty spots of Europe, and sought out the best hotels, the French chefs were on hand to contribute to the art of good living. The table manners and the French culinary style that had evolved in the taverns and restaurants of the Revolution were spread throughout the whole of the Western world for the aristocracy and upper middle class to savor.

THE CULINARY RENAISSANCE OF THE TWENTIETH CENTURY

Auguste Escoffier, dubbed the emperor of chefs by none other than Emperor William II of Germany, was for many years in charge of the kitchens of the Savoy Hotel in London, and subsequently of the Carlton Hotel, one of Europe's finest. For his services to the advancement of French cuisine worldwide, he was made a Chevalier of the Legion of Honor in 1920, and an Officer of the Legion in 1928.

He was a cook without equal who set about restructuring and codifying French cuisine, "adapting" it, as he said, to meet contemporary demands. His standardization of culinary science, which stands as a universal reference, was to permit a multiplication of the various formulae by which dishes are prepared. He made possible an expansion and diversification of the language of cooking.

This was particularly true in the area of sauces, and while it may seem such an abundance of gravies and concentrates is unnecessary, it underlines the importance of research, using subtle approaches to taste to draw out the predominant flavor of the main ingredient. This is not a far cry from the way in which cooks of the Middle Ages used spices as seasonings. The wheel had turned full circle.

And, having reached a peak, the only possible future was a decline followed by a renaissance. *Grande cuisine* became practically mummified, as though the work of the grand masters could not be surpassed, only reworked in an uninspired way.

One man proved an exception — the great chef and lover of literature, Edouard Nignon, who had worked in many prestigious restaurants in Europe and was once head chef to the tsar. Although less well known than other culinary stars, Nignon is acknowledged as the artist who put poetry back into food and as being the spiritual father of those who revolutionized cuisine some years later. He wrote three cook books, the finest being *L'Heptaméron des Gourmets ou les Délices de la Cuisine Française.*

Dramatic change could come about only if there was a revolt against Parisian centralism and the rigid standardization of international gastronomy. The first signs of change came at the start of the First World War. Marthe Allard, under the pseudonym of Pampille, published *Les Bons Plats de France* which highlighted regional specialties and featured simple, tasty recipes such as *pot-au-feu* (boiled beef) and *poule au pot* (boiled chicken) that were a direct contrast to the costly concoctions of *grande cuisine.*

A marvelous showcase for the specialties of every province was the eight-day fair of "regional gastronomy" held in Paris in 1923. The French began to discover the hidden and neglected treasures of their country. A literary figure, Maurice Edmond Sailland, known as Curnonsky, was to transform classical cuisine through his writings. This "Prince of Gastronomes" presented a knowledgeable interpretation of popular and regional dishes. The trend had been initiated — to culminate in the 1980s in a kind of culinary recasting — that would make French cuisine one of the most interesting in the world.

Now dietetics moved to center stage and became inextricably entwined with gastronomy. This "marriage" was promoted in part by the writings of the nutritionist and gourmet Edouard de Pomaine. Gastronomy wanted to become scientific.

It was more than a century since Grimod de La Reynière published a little guide to restaurants, inns and hotels; a successor was long overdue. *Guide Michelin* picked up the idea and classified hotels and restaurants nationwide according to merit, citing their

Vegetables and fruit, L. Valtat (1869–1952);
MUSEE DES BEAUX-ARTS, NANTES
Bell peppers (capsicums) and tomatoes are essential ingredients in *ratatouille*, the vegetable ragoût typical of Provençal cooking. It can be served on its own, or as an accompaniment to roasts, braised fish, and scrambled egg.

specialties and awarding them "stars." It meant that hitherto unknown establishments were "discovered" and put on the gastro-tourists' map. And culinary dynasties were founded in small family-operated inns: the Bocuse family at Collonges au Mont d'Or; the Haberlin family at Illhaeusen; the Daguins at Auch; and many others.

But a gastronomic revival was still waiting to happen. Other than an awakening of interest in regional specialties, by the end of the Second World War there was little that was new. However, in the 1960s dietitians and nutritionists were making their voices heard loud and clear; in the French mind was instilled the incompatibility of "good" and "healthy," of gastronomy and dietetics. What was needed was to reconcile good health and good cuisine, and this was achieved by one of the finest cooks of our time: Michel Guérard.

Guérard joined forces with journalists and food critics Henri Gault and Christian Millau to launch "La Nouvelle Cuisine." A profound change was underway: out went the old-fashioned and fossilized stereotypes from the period between Carême and Escoffier. In came the individual plate, decorated for each diner, that fulfilled each person's requirements. In the theories and recipes which he published in *La Grande Cuisine Minceur*, Guérard illustrated that he had succeeded in the prodigious feat of integrating dietetics, esthetics and health.

Supper draws to a close, Jules Grün (painted 1913);

Until the mid-nineteenth century supper was considered a suitably glittering ending to a ball. Restaurants then adopted the fashion, attracting theatergoers after the curtain came down. Many people continued to hold private suppers in their homes. They had, as E. Briffault wrote in *Paris à table,* "a certain smack of the forbidden fruit."

Guérard went back to the principle of respecting the flavor of each ingredient. He made use of the techniques of steaming and poaching, and of the modern wonder — the microwave oven. A new concept of sauces was developed. In the quest for lightness, flour was discarded as a thickening agent in favor of yogurt or reduced creams or butter, or very fine-textured vegetable purées. Mousses made a triumphant reappearance, their preparation made easy by the food processor. Light, succulent, delicate, airy — these are the words that best describe Nouvelle Cuisine.

Of course, there were chefs who took up Nouvelle Cuisine in an overzealous way; over-decoration of plates and curious combinations of foodstuffs are just two complaints. But it was not possible to liberate cuisine from 150 years of respectful repetition of the recipes of the old masters without some excesses occurring.

The exploratory period seems to have come to an end. We are now witnessing the establishment of a tradition that has been restored through a subtle blending of rustic cuisines with the rational approach of Nouvelle Cuisine. By drawing on our heritage, French cuisine has never looked better.

Apples and oranges, Paul Cézanne (1839–1906); MUSEE D'ORSAY, PARIS
In his still lifes Cézanne devoted hours to carefully arranging the various elements to achieve a perfect balance of color and form. One of his most well-known statements is, "When color has its greatest richness, then form has its plenitude." One young artist watching him work remarked, "One guessed it was a feast for the eye to him."

Picnic in the countryside near Strasbourg around 1750, Théophile Schuler (painted 1863); MUSÉE HISTORIQUE, STRASBOURG The word *pique-nique* was accepted by the Académie

rançaise in 1740.

SOUPS

In the beginning there was gruel. First food of the first farmers, in Europe it was fundamental even in the medieval centuries, and for many years subsequently the people of Northern Europe were loyal to this food, which could be made from barley, rye, oats, millet or wheat.

Hints of these cereal gruels, semiliquid in consistency and slowly simmered, can still be found in French cuisine. One of the popular dishes in the thirteenth and fourteenth centuries was frumenty, a gruel made from wheat and often milk, which gave it a better taste.

Today in certain regions of France these cereal soups can still be found, such as the *soupe à l'épeautre* of the Comtat Venaissin. *Epeautre*, or spelt, is an old-fashioned type of wheat, low in yield but high in flavor. This hearty soup is prepared with salted pork and *saucisses à la couenne* (sausages made with pork rind) and is allowed to cook for many hours.

From medieval times the word *soupe* originally meant a slice of bread over which the liquid soup was poured; it added body to the kind of dish that today we would call a soup. (In medieval England *soppes* or *soppys* designated the same thing). The slice of bread was sometimes toasted, in which case it was called a *tostée* (the same was used in England). To honor an invited guest it was customary to offer him or her a glass of wine in the base of which was one of these *tostées* — hence the expression "to drink a toast."

The term "potage" referred to a dish cooked in a pot, and at this time the pot was the principal, and sometimes only, utensil in the kitchen. *Potages liés*, of which one example is the *gravé*, were thickened with bread and corresponded to what would be called "ragoûts." This lasted until the Renaissance, and it was only about the seventeenth century that *soupes* and *potages* came to mean what they do today.

Be that as it may, soup was a basic food for the peasant class, the workers and the ordinary townsfolk. Slowly cooked in a pot hung over the fireplace the soup contained vegetables — a good proportion of root vegetables such as turnips, parsnips and carrots, plus leeks, onions and vegetable marrow (squash) — and a piece of meat if one could afford it. A rustic and common food, soup did not play an important part in *grande cuisine*, but sometimes it was refined having been puréed and enriched with cream and butter, and in this way it became an elegant food destined for delicate persons.

Saying grace, Jean Baptiste Siméon Chardin (1699–1779); THE HERMITAGE, LENINGRAD
A direct honesty and lack of sentimentality characterize Chardin's genre paintings.

The midday meal, Leon Lhermitte
(1844–1925);

The overhaul of farming practices
instigated by Olivier de Serres in the late
sixteenth and early seventeenth century
enlivened the diet of successive
generations. His dictum was, "A thriving
household depends on the use of seasonal
produce and the application of
commonsense."

Some soups achieved widespread fame. Without digressing on the *pot-au-feu*, the "boiled dinner" including both meat and vegetables which can be found in one form or another in all Western European countries, we should still spare a tender thought for the *poule au pot* dear to Henri IV. During a period of food shortages over a large part of his territory at the end of the sixteenth century, this worthy king expressed the wish that all his subjects could, at least once a week, on Sundays, add a boiling hen to their standard soup of root vegetables and herbs. Olivier de Serres, his advisor and the best agronomist of the time, initiated an enormous development in agriculture and livestock breeding in the country. The peasants found they were better off, and eventually they could at last regularly include a hen in their soup.

In later years, leading cooks were not above giving recipes for this kind of peasant dish, and in one of his books Menon passed on the secrets of the *garbure*, an outstanding soup from the Bearn region based on cabbage, pork and preserved goose or duck.

In the nineteenth century *grande cuisine* favored light consommés, which were like clear essences of meat or poultry, and the refined, creamy *velouté* soups. The soup was not required to be a meal in itself, it simply helped make the guest ready to enjoy the skillfully prepared dishes that would follow. And today the genuine peasant soup, thick with vegetables, meat, salted pork and bread, is rarely seen. Once, each region had its specialty. In the Southwest, as well as the *garbure* described above, there is a lighter soup known as *tourin*. It calls for onions, garlic, aromatic herbs, sometimes tomatoes, all cooked in good goose or duck fat, simmered in water, seasoned with vinegar and a pinch of sugar and thickened with eggs. These *tourins* are served, as they have been since the medieval era, in a soup tureen lined with thick slices of bread. In the Northeast there is the *potée*, a hearty blend of vegetables, including dried white beans with a variety of meats, chicken and pork amongst them. Along the shores of the Mediterranean, the famous *bouillabaisse* is a fish soup flavored with saffron and served with its *rouille*, a garlic mayonnaise spiced with chili. In Central France, and in particular in Auvergne, a cabbage soup with salted pork is favored.

Today soups have taken on a new character; they are light, full of flavor and freshness, and sometimes they are even eaten cold. They have become the overture to the symphony of the meal.

France still holds to tradition, especially in regard to eating habits. More than 48 per cent of French people eat soup in the evening, every day. The older generation believes that soup is the best and the most digestible food one can have before going to bed.

Porcelain tureen (eighteenth century); MUSEE NATIONAL DE CERAMIQUE, SEVRES
Sèvres soft-paste porcelain tableware varies from the charming, lightly handled decorative style (shown here) to the extraordinarily ornate one favored by Louis XVI. The introduction of hard-paste porcelain in 1769 saw the lighter touch prevail once more.

Preparing lunch, Nicolas-Bernard Lépicié (1735–84); MUSEE DES BEAUX-ARTS, RENNES
Cabbage, bacon, and onions — the typical ingredients for the robust *garbure* (cabbage and bacon soup).

Cream of asparagus soup (left); Pumpkin soup (right)

CREAM OF ASPARAGUS SOUP

Velouté d'asperges   Serves 4

This creamy soup is reminiscent of the refined creations of the eighteenth-century *grande cuisine*. It is thick and smooth, with a delicate flavor to suit the subtle tastes of the *grandes dames*. The use of asparagus, which was introduced into the *grande cuisine* of France under Italian influence during the Renaissance, was part of a progressive change in eating habits that gave more emphasis to vegetables, long considered the food of peasants.

1½ lb (750 g) small green asparagus spears
9 chervil sprigs
1½ tablespoons extra virgin olive oil
1 tablespoon arrowroot
1 cup (8 fl oz/250 ml) milk
salt and freshly ground pepper
6 pinches nutmeg
3 tablespoons thick crème fraîche *

Cut off 1¼ inches (3 cm) from the tip ends of the asparagus and reserve. Slice the remainder of the stalks into thin rounds. Rinse the chervil and pat dry. Heat the oil in a heavy-bottomed saucepan and cook the asparagus rounds for 5 minutes, stirring constantly, until just browned. Add the chervil sprigs and 4 cups (1 qt/1 l) of water. Bring to a boil. Reduce heat and simmer for 15 minutes.

Purée the asparagus mixture in a blender. Strain to remove the solids. Pour the mixture back into the pan, and add the arrowroot mixed with the milk. Add salt and pepper to taste and the nutmeg. Put the pan over low heat and bring the mixture to a boil. Add the asparagus tips and cook for about 4 minutes, stirring all the while, until the tips are just cooked and the soup is thick. Remove from the heat, add the *crème fraîche* and stir to mix. Serve at once. This soup is also good cold.

* *Crème fraîche:* Combine 1 cup (8 fl oz/250 ml) light (single) cream and 2 tablespoons buttermilk in a glass container. Cover and let stand at room temperature for 8–24 hours or until thick. Stir well, cover, and refrigerate for up to 10 days.

PUMPKIN SOUP

Potage à la citrouille   Serves 4–5

La *Maison Rustique*, published in the first half of the seventeenth century, is a treatise on agriculture and domestic economy for landowners. This soup appears in a section devoted to recipes and the various methods of preserving food. It is typical of the time in its emphasis on the *velouté* thickening and the fineness of the finish.

The vegetables of the New World, which had begun to make a tentative appearance in the sixteenth and seventeenth centuries, were by this time widely grown and consumed, except for the potato, which was little appreciated as yet, and the tomato, which was not well known outside the cuisine of Southern France.

> Take a piece of pumpkin, peel it and cut it into small pieces; cook it in a pot with water, salt, two cloves and a knob of butter; when it is cooked and very little liquid remains, crush any lumps that are left, with a wooden spoon; then add some milk, and when it begins to boil, take the pot off the fire; and have slices of bread ready in a dish, and pour the soup over them, and serve.

Iced tomato soup

1 garlic clove
1 whole clove
1 thyme sprig
4 cups (1 qt/1 l) milk
1½ lb (750 g) pumpkin flesh, cut into ¾ inch (2 cm) cubes
salt and freshly ground pepper
2 pinches grated nutmeg
2 pinches cayenne pepper
sage leaves for garnish

Tie the garlic, clove and thyme in a small square of cheesecloth (muslin).

Put the milk in a 4 qt (4 l) saucepan, add the garlic, clove and thyme in cheesecloth, the pumpkin cubes and a small amount of salt. Bring to a boil. Cover and cook over gentle heat for 30 minutes, stirring several times.

Discard the garlic, clove and thyme. Purée the soup in a food processor until very smooth.

Reheat the soup, adding the pepper, nutmeg and cayenne. Serve immediately garnished with sage leaves.

ICED TOMATO SOUP

Soupe glacée à la tomate   Serves 4

This light soup with its sharp flavor would evoke the tastes of medieval times, were it not for the main ingredient — tomato — which did not become popular in French cooking until after the Revolution. In 1789 the Provençaux brothers (in actual fact, brothers-in-law), who were in the service of the Prince of Conti, came to Paris from Marseilles and opened a restaurant in their own name. These two southerners revealed to Parisians the delights of *brandade de morue, aioli* and *bouillabaisse*, and helped to popularize the vegetables of the South, such as tomatoes.

2 lb (1 kg) ripe tomatoes, peeled, seeded and coarsely chopped
1 cup (8 fl oz/250 ml) chicken broth (stock)
4 tablespoons (2 fl oz/60 ml) extra virgin olive oil
2 tablespoons aged wine vinegar
1 garlic clove, crushed
salt and freshly ground pepper
4 teaspoons thick crème fraîche
12 small basil leaves

In a food processor, combine the tomatoes with the broth, oil, vinegar, garlic and salt and pepper. Process for 2 minutes at high speed, until the mixture is smooth. Refrigerate until ready to serve.

Serve this soup in deep plates, garnished with a teaspoon of *crème fraîche* and basil leaves.

CRETONÉE OF FRESH YOUNG PEAS

Cretonée de pois nouveaux   Serves 4

This recipe is taken from the *Ménagier de Paris*, which was written around 1390 by a wealthy Parisian. It appears in a section headed *Potages lians de chair*, that is to say, cream soups that had been pounded in a pestle, passed through a strainer, or "tammy," and thickened with eggs and bread — to some extent the forerunners of the eighteenth century's thickened soups.

> Cook them until they are soft enough to mash, and drain them, then take some good fresh cow's milk, and tell the girl who sells you the milk that she should not try to cheat you by adding water, for often they dilute their milk, and if it is not very fresh or if water has been added, it will curdle. And first of all bring this milk to the boil, and before you add anything to it, for this would make it curdle, too; then pound together the following: firstly ginger, to encourage the appetite, and saffron to make it yellow; another way of doing this is to use egg yolks to thicken, but the milk is more likely to curdle if you use egg yolks than if you use bread for thickening and saffron for coloring. And for this, if you wish to use bread as a thickening, it must be white non-leavened bread, and it has to be set to soak in a bowl with milk or meat broth, then pounded and strained through a sieve; and when your bread has been thus strained, but not your spices, add them all to boil with your peas; and when they are all cooked, then add your milk and the saffron. Alternatively, there is another way of thickening; that is, by using the peas or beans themselves, pounded and then passed through a sieve; and you can choose whichever method of thickening you prefer. For when you use egg yolks to thicken, you have to beat them together, strain them through the sieve and add them in a thin stream to the milk, after this has been well boiled, and has been drawn away from the heat, with the fresh peas or broad beans and the spices. The safest method is to take a little milk and mix it with the eggs in the bowl, and then add a little more and a little more again, so that the yolks are well diluted with plenty of milk, then turn it all into a pot, off the heat, and the mixture will not curdle. And if the mixture is too thick, thin it with a little meat broth. Having done this, you need to take young chickens in quarters, veal, or a small goose, cooked then fried, and put two or three pieces of meat in each bowl and the other preparation on top.

2 tablespoons (1 oz/30 g) butter
1 onion, chopped
1 lettuce heart (2 oz/60 g), finely shredded
4 cups (1 qt/1 l) chicken broth (stock)
2 lb (1 kg) fresh peas, shelled, or broad beans
salt and freshly ground pepper

The butter maker, Jean François Millet (1814–1875); THE LOUVRE, PARIS
Buttermilk, the liquid that remains after churning cream, is used commercially in France as an emulsifier in pastries and desserts.

⅓ cup (3 fl oz/90 ml) thick crème fraîche
4 chervil sprigs

Melt the butter in a 4 qt (4 l) saucepan. Add the onion and brown gently over low heat for 2 minutes, stirring constantly. Add the lettuce and stir for another 2 minutes.

Pour in the chicken broth, and bring to a boil. Add the peas and cook for about 20 minutes, until tender. Season with salt and pepper.

When the peas are cooked, remove ¼ cup of peas. Purée the remaining peas and liquid in a blender. Strain, and return the soup to the pan. Reheat to a boil. Add the *crème fraîche*, stir well and remove from the heat.

Pour the soup into a tureen, garnish with the reserved peas and the chervil and serve hot.

Cretonée of fresh young peas

WINTER SOUP WITH THREE VEGETABLES

Soupe d'hiver aux trois légumes   Serves 4

From the nineteenth century on, vegetable soup was the typical dish to begin the evening meal in modest and middle-class French homes. Leeks, potatoes, celery, carrots, turnips, and squash made it a dish for winter. Among the peasants it sometimes constituted the entire meal, perhaps embellished with a plain piece of bacon or a sliver of butter, depending on the custom of the region. This contemporary version is lighter and more refined, but what it loses in substance it gains in delicacy of taste and texture.

2 tablespoons extra virgin olive oil
1 celery heart (6½ oz/200 g), cut into thin rounds
13 oz (410 g) potatoes, peeled and cut into

¼ inch (5 mm) cubes or coarsely grated
1½ lb (750 g) pumpkin flesh, cut into ½ inch (1 cm) cubes
salt

Heat the oil in a 4 qt (4 l) nonaluminum pot. Add the celery heart and cook over gentle heat for 2 minutes, stirring constantly with a wooden spoon. Add the potatoes and cook for 1 minute. Add the pumpkin cubes and 2 cups (16 fl oz/500 ml) water. Add salt and bring to a boil. Cover the pot and simmer for about 40 minutes, stirring from time to time, until the potatoes disintegrate.

Pour the soup into a tureen and serve very hot. Add pepper before eating. This soup is also excellent cold.

Winter soup with three vegetables (left); Chilled zucchini soup (right)

Still life with vegetables, Henri-Horace Roland de la Porte (1724–1793); MUSEE DES BEAUX-ARTS, ROUEN The pumpkin is grown in southern France and harvested in October for use throughout the winter months.

CHILLED ZUCCHINI SOUP

Potage froid aux courgettes   Serves 4

This soup, redolent of the freshness and fragrance of summer, contains the flavors of the Midi, Basil and olive oil, tomatoes and zucchini (courgettes), bound together with the delicious flavor of garlic, eaten cold, demonstrate the ability of modern French cooking to orchestrate variations on the age-old garlic and vegetable soups typical of the provinces south of the Loire.

4 young garlic cloves
12 large basil leaves
3 tablespoons extra virgin olive oil
salt
13 oz (410 g) ripe tomatoes, peeled, seeded and
 coarsely chopped

1 ¼ lb (600 g) zucchini (courgettes)
2 tablespoons basil leaves, minced or shredded

In a stockpot, combine the garlic, 12 large basil leaves, 1 tablespoon of the oil and some salt. Add 4 cups (1 qt/1 l) of water and the tomatoes. Bring to a boil.

Coarsely grate the zucchini in a food processor. Add to the stockpot and cook, covered, over gentle heat for 40 minutes.

Allow to cool a little. Blend the soup until smooth. Set aside to cool completely. Cover and refrigerate.

At serving time divide the soup among 4 bowls, drizzle the remaining olive oil over each serving and scatter with the minced basil.

The butler's table, Jean Baptiste Siméon Chardin (1699–1779); THE LOUVRE, PARIS Chardin was the finest still-life and genre painter of the French eighteenth century. He drew

gether the simplest elements — a silver-plated spirit warmer, a tureen, oil, and vinegar bottles — and rendered them with great delicacy of touch.

APPETIZERS

As the French name for appetizers, *entrées*, implies, in French cuisine they are dishes served at the start of a meal, before the main courses. The term *entrée* became popularized in the sixteenth and seventeenth centuries, but in a slightly different context — the explanation for which requires a brief detour via the history of meal service and the style known as *à la française*. From the medieval period to the middle of the nineteenth century, meals in France were not served as an ordered series of dishes, as they are today, since we adopted the *service à la russe* style. At that time the various dishes were presented together as a composite group, each group being a *service*. Anything from three to six *services*, or even more, could make up a meal, and each *service* represented a different stage of the meal. For the first the table was set with a number of dishes of all kinds, and guests helped themselves to whatever they wanted to taste. The table was then cleared, reset with the dishes of the second *service*, and so on. During medieval banquets in the interval between two *services* and while the table was being set, there were amusements in the form of musicians, singers, dancers, and other distractions, for the entertainment of the guests. Such spectacles were called *entremets*, and this word was absorbed into culinary terminology, designating dishes that linked two *services* (or two principal dishes), before it came to mean what it does today, a sweet dish served at the end of a meal.

Let us imagine that we have been invited to a formal dinner in the seventeenth century. The star of each *service*, the focus around which the secondary dishes are arranged, is the largest dish. The first *service* includes *potages* and *entrées*: along both sides of the table are magnificent soup tureens containing soups made from costly ingredients; around them are arrayed small *entrées* — pâtés, truffled chickens, *fricandeaux* (larded roasts of veal), and other substantial delicacies. In the center of the table is the *grande entrée* composed of two huge roasts flanked by various cutlets and appropriate sauces. Finally, surrounding all these dishes, the *hors d'oeuvre*, little garnishes to enhance the magnificence of the whole presentation — quail, stuffed pigeons, and chickens, braised lettuce and veal sweetbreads. The second *service* replicates the first: the soup tureens are replaced by immense platters of roast meats — poultry, meat, and all kinds of game. Taking the place of the *grande entrée* are *entremets* consisting of pâtés, *blanc-manger*, *galantines*, asparagus and other delights. Encircling all this are the *hors d'oeuvre*, this time including

Wedding feast at Yport (detail), Albert-Auguste Fourié (1854–?); MUSEE DES BEAUX-ARTS, ROUEN
The wedding feasts of the nobility and French royalty frequently lasted several days; so, too, those of the rural community, at which many meat dishes and types of cake were served. In recent times festivities have become less protracted affairs, with great emphasis being placed on the size and design of the cake, many regions having their own specialty.

Still life with salad, Edouard Vuillard
(1869–1940); MUSEE D'ORSAY, PARIS
The word "salad" is derived from the
Latin *sal* (salt). The best-known salad
dressing of olive oil, salt, and vinegar is
equally ancient in its origins.

morels, skewers of grilled meats, artichokes, chicken pies, and stuffed cocks' combs. The
same arrangement is repeated for all the other *services*, including the final one in which
a number of sweet dishes is offered. Sitting around the table the guests eat whatever is
in reach, and there are no two plates of the same dish. Anyone who wants to taste a dish
that is not accessible has to ask one of the waiters for help.

The costly splendor of the *service à la française* gave way, in about 1840–50, to the
more efficient and economical *service à la russe* in which the dishes are served individually
to each guest according to a set order. But didn't the great Carême himself say that the
service à la française was more elegant and magnificent?

The words referring to dishes in the *à la française* arrangement have remained with
us; menus today use the terms *entrées* and *hors d'oeuvre*, but with different meanings.

The *hors d'oeuvre* had changed dramatically throughout the centuries. In the *service
à la française* they were little garnishes. However, previously, the Renaissance writer
Rabelais, a lover of good food, mentions *hors d'oeuvre* as being served at the very end
of the meal, after dessert, somewhat in the fashion of savories in a classic English meal.
He called them *des éperons bachiques* or bacchic spurs. They must have been savory
indeed to induce such thirst! However, in the classical centuries which followed, *hors
d'oeuvre* remained unimportant side garnishes to the various *services* of the meal. When
the *service à la russe* became popular, the *hors d'oeuvre* began their successful career
which was to last over a century.

In the late 1900s, in every respectable bourgeois household, as in every restaurant with any pretensions to excellence, the *hors d'oeuvre* became an important course. They were served after the soup and before the appetizers, supposedly to stimulate the guest's appetite.

They were divided by the chefs into two categories: the cold *hors d'oeuvres*, more suitable for lunches, and hot *hors d'oeuvres* preferred for evening meals. A formal dinner would include both. Hot *hors d'oeuvres* were also called *entrées volantes* (flying *entrées*) or *petites entrées* (small *entrées*). As their French name implies ("out of the main work") they were considered an outside element in the general pattern of the meal.

It is almost impossible to describe the infinite variety of foods served under that name. It includes anything edible, from vegetables and fruit to shellfish, fish, meats, and poultry, breads, pastries, cheese, and eggs. Either eaten raw, under the generic name of *crudités*, or cooked in a variety of ways. Up to this century, ingredients could include marinades of fruit, oysters, or seaweed. The latter disappeared from the tables until recently, when young chefs began to rediscover the qualities of this healthy sea vegetable.

These culinary creations were light, elaborate, and small. A great emphasis was on pattern, color, and shape. All the classic cookbooks insisted on the need for original and unusual presentations. Edible garden flowers such as nasturtiums, borage, chrysanthemum, or daisies were used to decorate and to add piquancy to the taste. Small sets of silver and crystal dishes or antique porcelain were considered the suitable setting for such delicacies.

But since these foods were meant to stimulate rather than quench the appetite, they had to be light, delicate, and small in size. In the 1930s, Edouard de Pomaine who was

The four elements, or winter, Sébastien Stoskopff (1596/7–1657);
MUSEE DES BEAUX-ARTS, STRASBOURG
Blessed with diverse provisions from earth, sea, and sky, French cuisine has evolved into one of the most sophisticated and varied in the world. Just add fire.

RVSTICVS IN GALLIA.

CV.

French peasant, print from "Habitus praecipuorum popularum," Jost Amman (1577); NATIONAL LIBRARY, MADRID
The most common breeds of duck in France are the Nantes and the Barbary. A cross of these two — the mulard — is reared for *foie gras.* Also highly prized today, though less available, is the Rouen. Its special flavor is due to the fact that it is not bled like the others but smothered so that the blood remains in the muscles.

a nutritionist, gourmet, marvelous cook and a good food writer insisted that "you should not fill your guests' stomach with *hors d'oeuvre,* they have to be able to appreciate the main course!"

Until the advent of the Nouvelle Cuisine, a great array of *hors d'oeuvre* was considered elegant. Restaurants offered laden trolleys where *crudités,* scampi, pâtés, and croquettes, hot savories and smoked fish, charcuterie and egg dishes were arranged in magnificent pyramids with a great deal of color.

In the home, the lady of the house devoted much time and imagination to her tray of *hors d'oeuvres:* it was a sign of distinction. The most distinguished of all being caviar.

Caviar was not a novelty. Known in France since the fifteenth century, it is thought to have been introduced via Turkey, and was at the time considered as worthy Lenten fare. It was eaten as a salad, with oil and vinegar, or, as today, on toast with lemon juice. A seventeenth-century recipe even recommends it being fried with herbs. Late in the nineteenth century the craze for caviar as a luxury food began in earnest and the French decided to produce their own.

Many sturgeon were found in the estuary of the Gironde, above Bordeaux, and the Girondins started to collect the eggs, salt them and process them as the Iranians and the Russians from the Caspian Sea had done. French caviar was a success. Unhappily it led to overfishing and exploitation. In the 1950s there were practically no sturgeon left. Today efforts are being made by the local fisheries, and there is hope to produce caviar once more in a few years' time.

In more modest ways, *hors d'oeuvre* continued to be popular throughout the years. Every restaurant, however unpretentious, had its *hors d'oeuvre variés.* But they had lost much of their lavishness to become the little dishes that one nibbles at the very start of a meal, although today the dish of radishes with butter, the slice of sausage or the piece of sardine in oil, is gradually disappearing from our tables, leaving the *entrée* to take the principal role.

The meals served in the first part of the twentieth century, and to a certain extent up to the Second World War, were far more extravagant and rich than today. The formal meal included: soup, *hors d'oeuvre, entrées,* a fish dish, a poultry dish, a meat roast, vegetables, a salad, cheese, desserts, and fruit. For men, and to a certain extent for women, a good appetite was an admired quality. Needless to say, the ideal figure was somewhat heavier than our contemporary emaciated ideal. You could eat both *hors d'oeuvre* and *entrées* and still be hungry for the rest of the meal. Things began to change after the Second World War.

First, the "apéritif," or before-meal drinks, gained much popularity. The drinks, often strong spirits like Scotch whisky, or the Mediterranean *pastis,* were served with finger foods. These have replaced the *hors d'oeuvre.* Nuts, morsels of cheese, olives, and pickles or savories are served on the coffee table and have lost their place at the meal. The *entrée* became the first course. At the same time, fashion and tradition moved on. A lighter way of eating was favored and acquired a new status with the advent of Nouvelle Cuisine. The *hors d'oeuvre* became superfluous, as it unbalanced the pattern of the meal. Nevertheless, today many good chefs offer what they call a *mise en bouche* (preparing the palate). These are tiny savory dishes, intended to stimulate the guests' appetite and curiosity about the meal to come. It can be one mussel, followed by a quail's egg and just a hint of ratatouille, the quantities never exceeding a teaspoonful!

Entrées can be based on fish or shellfish, eggs, game, or poultry. They should be light, so as not to ruin guests' appetites. Pâtés, *tourtes* and terrines also have an important part to play. Furred or feathered game or even meat from more modest domestic animals go into their preparation, lending them an infinite variety, according to the province of origin. Flavored with spices or aromatic herbs, with Cognac or armagnac or other spirits, with or without truffles, cooked in a pastry case or not, such preparations have recipes that can be traced back to the 1300s. In contrast, *entrées* based on vegetables, such as artichokes and asparagus, and including mixed salads, take their cue from the Renaissance and Italian influences. Quiches, which are said to have seen the light of day in Lorraine, are tarts with a filling based on eggs and salt pork, just as they were described 500 years ago in *Le Ménagier de Paris*. And in Nouvelle Cuisine, *entrées* were an important area of invention and innovation: vegetable tarts, savory *bavaroises*, tangy mousses, chilled salads tossed with warm dressings, all interpreted for a whole range of tastes.

A copper pot, spice box, and eggs, Jean Baptiste Siméon Chardin (1699–1779); THE LOUVRE, PARIS
The "props" used in this picture appear together or separately in several of Chardin's works. Only the most basic, staple provisions are ever included; bread, eggs, raw fish, meat, and vegetables.

Spring table, Henri E. Lesidaner (1862–1939); INTERNATIONAL GALLERY OF MODERN ART, CA' PESARO, VENICE
The Neo-Impressionists continued the love affair with painting outdoor settings.

SWISS CHARD AND SPINACH PIE

Tourte aux blettes   Serves 6

This is a recipe from the fourteenth century given in the *Ménagier de Paris*. It began life as a middle-class dish cooked in pastry and liberally flavored with ginger. For centuries herb or spinach *tourtes* were a staple peasant dish. Rétif de la Bretonne, a writer, journalist and chronicler of the second half of the eighteenth century, refers frequently to these tarts or pies, which were served at the family table on his father's farm. Dishes of this kind are still found today in the regions from Bourgogne to Haute Provence.

> Take four handfuls of Swiss chard [silverbeet], two handfuls of parsley, one of chervil, a sprig of fennel and two handfuls of spinach, and pick through them and wash them in cold water, then chop them very finely; then pound two different kinds of cheese, that is to say, some soft and some medium cheese; then add to this some eggs, both yolks and whites, and pound them with the cheese; then add the herbs to the mortar and pound everything together; and then add some ground spice mixture. Or instead of this you could first of all crush in the mortar two little pieces of ginger, and on top of this pound your cheeses, eggs and herbs, then sprinkle over the top of this herb mixture some grated old cheese, or similar, and carry it to the oven, and turn it into a pastry shell, and eat it while hot.

1¾ cups (6½ oz/200 g) all-purpose (plain) flour
⅓ cup (3½ fl oz/100 ml) extra virgin olive oil
4 pinches salt
3½ oz (100 g) Swiss chard (silverbeet)
3½ oz (100 g) spinach leaves
1 small (2 oz/60 g) onion

1 small leek, white part only
½ oz (15 g) fresh dill
½ oz (15 g) fresh chervil
½ oz (15 g) fresh parsley
⅓ cup (3½ oz/100 g) fresh ricotta
2 eggs
½ cup (2 oz/60 g) freshly grated Parmesan cheese
salt and freshly ground pepper
1 tablespoon extra virgin olive oil

Sift the flour onto your work surface. Make a well in the center, and add the oil, about 4 tablespoons (2 fl oz/60 ml) water and the salt. Work the dough quickly until it forms a ball. Refrigerate for 2 hours.

Preheat the oven to 400°F (200°C/Gas 6). Remove the dough from the refrigerator. Combine the Swiss chard, spinach, onion, leek and herbs in the bowl of a food processor. Run it for 30 seconds — the herbs should not be too finely chopped. Add the ricotta, eggs, Parmesan and salt and pepper and process for 10 seconds.

Divide the dough into 2 balls and roll them out separately. Butter a nonstick 9½ inch (24 cm) pie pan and line it with half the dough. Pour in the herb mixture. Top with the remaining dough and crimp the edges to seal in the filling. Using a pastry brush, coat the whole surface of the pie with olive oil.

Bake the pie in the preheated oven for 40 minutes. Transfer to a serving dish and serve hot or warm.

PASTA WITH PISTOU

Pâtes au pistou   Serves 6

In comparison to the Italians, the French came late to the appreciation of pasta. It did not become widespread as an ingredient throughout the country until the nineteenth century, and even then it was largely used to thicken the soups that simmered in the kitchens of the lower middle classes, or to make filling and inexpensive mixtures for working-class families. Certainly, we find recipes in the eighteenth century for *timbales* of macaroni, and other dishes of a similar nature inspired by Italian cuisine. But not until the twentieth century was pasta given a respectable place in the *grande cuisine* of France, and it was not until the advent of Nouvelle Cuisine that the great chefs produced some truly outstanding creations with pasta.

Pistou comes from Provence and has its origins in the Italian *pesto*. This olive oil and basil-based mixture is also used to flavor the summer vegetable soups of the Southeast.

3½ oz (100 g) fresh basil leaves
3 garlic cloves, quartered
⅓ cup (1½ oz/45 g) pine nuts
½ cup (2 oz/60 g) freshly grated Parmesan cheese
⅓ cup (3½ fl oz/100 ml) extra virgin olive oil
salt and freshly ground pepper
1 lb (500 g) fresh tagliatelle
2 tablespoons (1 oz/30 g) butter

In a blender, combine the basil, garlic, pine nuts, cheese, oil and salt and pepper. Blend for 2 minutes into a green purée. This is the *pistou*.

Cook the pasta in boiling salted water in a large stockpot until *al dente* — approximately 3 to 5 minutes. Drain the pasta, reserving about ⅓ cup (3 fl oz/90 ml) of the cooking water.

Place the pasta in a deep dish. Scatter with the butter and coat with the *pistou*. Mix well, adding a few spoonfuls of the cooking water if the pasta tends to stick. Serve at once, with additional grated Parmesan.

Note: The pine nuts may be replaced by walnuts, and half the Parmesan by very finely grated aged *pecorino* cheese. Other varieties of fresh or dried pasta such as *spaghetti alla chitarra* (square, matchstick-shaped strands), *trenette* or *linguine* can be served the same way.

Swiss chard and spinach pie (left); Pasta with pistou (right)

55

ARTICHOKES IN OLIVE OIL

Artichauts à la barigoule   Serves 4

Menon published *La Cuisinière Bourgeoise* in 1746. As the title indicates, it is a book written for the middle class, and the recipes in it are simpler and more rustic than those of the same author, published around the same time, concerning the *grande cuisine*. These artichokes are presented in *La Cuisinière Bourgeoise* as a garnish for roasts and other meat dishes. The recipe survives almost unchanged in most present-day cookbooks.

Take three or four artichokes, according to their size or to the size of your *entremets* dish, cut off the green underneath and half the leaves, put them in a pot with stock or water, two spoonfuls of good oil, a little salt and pepper, an onion, two roots, a bouquet garni; let them cook, and the sauce reduce to very little; when they are cooked, and there is no sauce left, let them fry for a minute or so in the oil to brown a little; then turn them into a pie dish with the oil left in the pot, take out the fibrous part at the base of the leaves, and cover them with the lid of the pie dish, very hot, and put some hot coals in the lid to broil [grill] the leaves; if you have a hot oven, they will be even better; when they are all broiled to a nice color, serve them with a sauce made of oil, vinegar, salt and coarse pepper.

12 small purple artichokes (about 4 oz/125 g each)

½ lemon

¼ cup (2 fl oz/60 ml) extra virgin olive oil

2 oz (60 g) pork fat or salt pork, finely chopped

2 small onions, minced

2 garlic cloves, minced

1 bay leaf, halved

2 thyme sprigs, crumbled

⅓ cup (3 fl oz/90 ml) dry white wine

salt and freshly ground pepper

Cut off the artichoke stalks ¾ inch (2 cm) from the heart; remove the tough leaves and cut the tips off the remaining leaves ¾ inch (2 cm) above the heart. Trim the hearts and stalks and rub them with the half lemon.

Heat the oil in a deep nonaluminum casserole just large enough to hold the artichokes. Add the bacon and cook for 1 minute. Add the garlic and onions and cook, stirring, for 5 minutes but do not let them brown. Add the artichokes, bay leaf and thyme. Stir and brown for 2 minutes. Add the wine and ⅓ cup (3 fl oz/90 ml) water. Season with salt and pepper. Cover and cook over very low heat for about 45 minutes, or until the artichokes are quite soft and coated with the thick cooking juices. Serve warm.

Still life with kettle, Paul Cézanne (1839–1906); MUSÉE D'ORSAY, PARIS Very large kettles made of earthenware or copper were known in ancient times; in France they were called *coquemars.*

Artichokes in olive oil (left); Celeriac rémoulade (right)

CELERIAC RÉMOULADE

Céleri rémoulade   Serves 6

Like *saucisson-beurre* (sliced sausage with bread and butter) and radishes with salt, celeriac (celery root) *rémoulade* was an archetypal *hor d'oeuvre* in restaurants popular with the ordinary people during the 1930s. It is a delicious way of eating this rather unpromising tuber, which generally used to be destined for the soup pot. When the French spoke of *crudités* it meant for most of them the inseparable pairing of celeriac *rémoulade* with grated carrots in a vinaigrette sauce. It took the recent changes in taste and cooking methods to develop the range of vegetables that nowadays can be served raw.

1 head celeriac (celery root) (about 1½ lb/750 g)
3 tablespoons lemon juice
salt
1 egg yolk
1 tablespoon Dijon mustard
⅓ cup (3 fl oz/90 ml) peanut (groundnut) oil

salt and freshly ground pepper
1 tablespoon lemon juice or wine vinegar
2 tablespoons light (single) cream

Peel the celeriac; cut it by hand or in a food processor into fine julienne. Boil water in a large nonaluminum saucepan; add the lemon juice and some salt. Put in the celeriac and when the water returns to a boil remove the saucepan from the heat. Drain the celeriac and refresh under running water. Drain again in a strainer, then dry it in a cloth.

Prepare the sauce. Whisk the egg yolk and the mustard together in a bowl. Keep whisking as you add the oil in a thin stream, until you have a thick mayonnaise. Add salt, pepper and lemon juice and mix again. Mix in the cream and continue to whisk until the sauce is creamy.

Place the celeriac in a large bowl. Add the sauce and mix well. Refrigerate until ready to serve, sprinkled with black pepper.

57

VEGETABLES À LA GRECQUE

Légumes à la grecque   Serves 6

The earliest *à la grecque* recipes featured onions and mushrooms. These small vegetables, which we could almost class as preserves in their lemon and oil marinade, flavored with coriander seeds, were part of the large range of *hors d'oeuvres* of the time. They make a delicious light appetizer and are a classic of twentieth-century cuisine.

3 purple artichokes (about 5 oz/155 g each)
½ lemon
12 scallions (spring onions)
18 button mushrooms (champignons)
12 cauliflower florets
1 small red bell pepper (capsicum)
1 large stick celery, cut into 6 pieces

¾ cup (6½ fl oz/200 ml) lemon juice
⅓ cup plus 1 tablespoon (3½ fl oz/100 ml) extra virgin olive oil
½ teaspoon coarsely ground white pepper
½ teaspoon fennel seeds
1 tablespoon coriander seeds
salt

Cut off the stalk of each artichoke ¾ inch (2 cm) from the heart; remove the tough leaves and cut off the tips of the remaining leaves ¾ inch (2 cm) above the heart. Trim the hearts and the stalks and rub them with the half lemon. Cut each heart into 6 pieces. Blanch in salted water for 5 minutes, then drain.

Peel the onions and blanch for 5 minutes in salted water. Drain and set aside with the artichokes.

Cut the stems off the mushrooms. Blanch the caps for 1 minute. Blanch the cauliflower and the celery the same way. Cut the bell pepper flesh into small dice.

In a nonaluminum saucepan, combine the lemon juice, oil, white pepper, fennel and coriander seeds, some salt and 2 cups (16 fl oz/500 ml) water. Bring to a boil. Add the artichokes, onions, mushrooms, cauliflower and celery and cook for 10 minutes. Add the bell pepper and cook for a further 5 minutes.

Remove the vegetables with a skimmer and transfer them to a deep dish. On high heat, reduce the cooking liquid to a syrupy consistency. Pour over the vegetables and let cool completely before serving.

Vegetables prepared this way may be kept in the refrigerator for 24 hours.

CHICKEN LIVER TERRINE

Terrine de foie de volailles   Serves 6–8

A terrine is like a pâté without a crust, cooked, as the name suggests, in an earthenware or ovenproof china terrine. There are numerous varieties, and each French region has its specialty and every cook his or her own preference and secret recipe. Recipes for terrines are found in the earliest French cookbooks, and they use all types of meat, poultry and fish.

Not only is the terrine a popular appetizer, in former times it was also a major ingredient of mid-morning snacks, elaborate breakfasts, picnics and travel provisions.

Vegetables à la grecque

Chicken liver terrine

3 shallots, minced

2 tablespoons (1 oz/30 g) butter

1½ lb (750 g) chicken livers, cleaned

10 oz (315 g) boneless chicken breast

3½ oz (100 g) raw ham

⅓ cup (3 fl oz/90 ml) port

2½ tablespoons (1 fl oz/30 ml) Armagnac

2 eggs

2 garlic cloves, crushed

4 pinches ground cinnamon

6 pinches thyme leaves

1 teaspoon fine (table) salt

1 teaspoon finely and freshly ground pepper

2 tablespoons peanut (groundnut) oil

6 bay leaves

Preheat the oven to 350°F (180°C/Gas 4).

Put the shallots in a small saucepan with half the butter and 1 tablespoon water. Place the pan over gentle heat and sauté the shallots, stirring for 5 minutes. Set aside.

Melt the remaining butter in a nonstick 9½ inch (24 cm) skillet. Add the livers and cook for 1 minute over medium heat. Remove from the heat, and let cool slightly. Cut the livers into ½ inch (1 cm) cubes; put them into a bowl and add the shallots.

Cut the chicken breast and ham into pieces and put them into a food processor. Process at medium speed and then add the port, Armagnac, eggs, garlic, cinnamon and thyme. Add the salt and pepper and mix thoroughly. Stir into the liver and shallot mixture, mixing well.

Oil an 11 inch/1¼ qt (28 cm/1.25 l) cast-iron or porcelain terrine. Pack with the mixture, patting it down well. Brush the surface with the oil and arrange the bay leaves on top. Cover the terrine, put it into the hot oven and cook for 1½ hours. Uncover and cook for 15 minutes, until the top of the terrine is browned.

Set aside to cool completely. Cover and refrigerate for at least 12 hours before serving.

Serve the terrine at room temperature, sliced and accompanied with toast and a green salad dressed with walnut oil.

Ballotine of duckling with chestnuts (top); Green asparagus with soft-boiled eggs (bottom)

BALLOTINE OF DUCKLING WITH CHESTNUTS

Ballottine de cannette aux marrons   Serves 6

The exquisite *ballotine* reached the height of its sophistication in the classical French cuisine that flourished in the eighteenth century. *Ballotines* have always been part of the great French culinary repertoire. In times past they were merely one of the many dishes that made up each course of a meal. Today a *ballotine* like this one can perfectly well serve as the main dish for lunch or dinner.

*1 duckling (about 3 lb/1.5 kg), boned and
    butterflied, legs and wings reserved*

3 tablespoons muscat or Madeira

salt and freshly ground pepper

1 teaspoon (5 g) powdered (2 leaves) unflavored gelatin

10 oz (315 g) boned chicken breast

5 oz (155 g) cooked ham

1 egg

2 pinches Chinese five-spice powder

6 pinches freshly grated nutmeg

2 shallots, minced

3 tablespoons minced flat-leaved (Italian) parsley

6½ oz (200 g) shelled chestnuts

2 teaspoons peanut (groundnut) oil

Preheat the oven to 350°F (180°C/Gas 4).

Lay the duck out flat on your work surface and brush it all over with 1 tablespoon of the muscat. Season with salt and pepper. Set aside while you prepare the stuffing.

Pour the remaining 2 tablespoons of muscat into a small nonaluminum saucepan. Sprinkle the gelatin over it and set aside to soften. Cut the chicken breast and the ham into cubes and put them into a food processor. Process on high speed for 1 minute. Add the egg, five-spice powder, nutmeg and salt and pepper to taste. Mix for 30 seconds.

Set the muscat and gelatin over low heat and heat gently. Mix until dissolved and then pour the mixture into the food processor. Process for 10 seconds.

Combine the shallots and parsley and sprinkle the mixture over the flesh of the duckling. Put the stuffing in the center of the bird in the form of a wide roll, and insert the chestnuts into this, pointed ends down. Place the wings and legs inside the duckling. Close up the 2 sides of the bird and sew the 2 ends with white cotton thread. Oil the bird lightly all over.

Put the *ballotine*, seam side down, in a cast-iron casserole. Place in the oven and cook without disturbing for 1¾ hours.

Transfer the *ballotine* to a serving dish. Remove the fat that will have risen to the surface of the sauce, and pour the sauce into a sauceboat.

Serve the duckling hot, cut into slices, with steamed vegetables, or cold, with a salad in season.

GREEN ASPARAGUS WITH SOFT-BOILED EGGS

Asperges vertes aux oeufs mollets   Serves 2

Here is a dish that would have pleased the French gourmets of the Renaissance, for at that time the tender asparagus was a culinary novelty. Since then, the appearance of fresh asparagus on our tables announces that spring is here. Seventeenth-century cooks recommended that asparagus be eaten slightly crunchy — *al dente*, as the Italians say. Later, it was preferred soft, with a longer cooking time. Whether you like it, as Marcel Proust did, with a *mousseline* sauce, or prefer *hollandaise* or vinaigrette, it is among the finest vegetables in French cooking.

When vegetables are presented *en asperge* it generally means they are in the form of young shoots or sprouts, and the term is usually applied to the first-picked vegetables gathered in the spring.

2 lb (1 kg) green asparagus
2 tablespoons (1 oz/30 g) butter
2 tablespoons freshly grated Parmesan cheese
4 eggs

Cut off each asparagus spear 2¾ inches (7 cm) from the end of each tip. Keep the stalks for another use.

Cook the asparagus tips for 7 minutes in boiling salted water and then drain. Discard the water and return the asparagus to the saucepan; add the butter and roll the tips around in it. Add the Parmesan and mix again; cover the saucepan.

Bring some water to a boil in another saucepan and put in the eggs. Boil for 5 minutes, refresh under running water. Shell the eggs.

Divide the asparagus tips between 2 plates. Place the eggs in the center of the plate and serve immediately.

To eat, break the eggs with a fork; the yolks will run out and coat the asparagus. Add pepper to taste.

Note: For the eggs to cook perfectly they must be at room temperature, not chilled, before cooking.

The basket of eggs, Henri-Horace Roland de la Porte (1724–1793); THE LOUVRE, PARIS In the seventeenth century, the famous chef Pierre François de la Varenne wrote a cookbook containing sixty recipes for eggs.

ENDIVE WITH CRISPY BACON AND MUSHROOMS

Frisée aux lardons et aux champignons croustillants

Serves 4

Green salad with bacon, and more particularly dandelion salad, is a peasant dish from the North of France. It is eaten not as an appetizer but halfway through the meal. Or, accompanied by potatoes, it can serve as supper. It is South of the Loire that salad was traditionally served at the start of the meal, a custom that in recent years has been generally adopted throughout the country. The two traditions have mingled and today endive and bacon has become a classic appetizer, light and appealing.

2 shallots, minced
1 teaspoon hot mustard
1 teaspoon sherry vinegar
3 tablespoons extra virgin olive oil
salt and freshly ground pepper

8 very thin slices smoked bacon
2 tablespoons peanut (groundnut) oil
4 large, very fresh mushrooms, thinly sliced
12 quail eggs (optional)
1 large head curly endive, washed and dried

Combine the shallots, mustard, vinegar, olive oil and salt and pepper in a salad bowl. Mix the vinaigrette well.

Cut the bacon into ½ inch (1 cm) strips. Brown over high heat in a nonstick 11 inch (28 cm) skillet, stirring constantly. Set aside on a plate.

Put 1 tablespoon of the peanut oil in the pan and brown the mushrooms with a little salt, stirring all the time. Set aside. Add the remaining peanut oil and fry the quail eggs.

Add the endive to the vinaigrette and mix well.

Divide the salad among 4 plates. Garnish with the mushrooms and place the quail eggs in the center. Scatter the crisp bacon over, and serve at once.

Endive with crispy bacon and mushrooms

TERRINE OF DUCK WITH HAZELNUTS

Terrine de canard aux noisettes   Serves 6

Terrines are another way of preserving meat or poultry for several weeks. Duck terrine must have been particularly good in autumn, when the birds were in season and fat and succulent. In fact, the hazelnuts in this recipe give it a subtle flavor that evokes the end of summer.

3 tablespoons milk

3 tablespoons Cognac

1 teaspoon (5 g) powdered (2 leaves) unflavored gelatin

3½ oz (100 g) shelled hazelnuts

¾ cup (1½ oz/45 g) fresh breadcrumbs

1 boned duck breast (about 8 oz/250 g), skinned

salt

1 teaspoon finely and freshly ground pepper

6½ oz (200 g) boned chicken breast

3½ oz (100 g) cooked ham

½ teaspoon ground allspice

1 garlic clove, crushed

1 shallot, crushed

1 egg

1 tablespoon peanut oil

Preheat the oven to 350°F (180°C/Gas 4).

In a small nonaluminum saucepan, combine the milk and Cognac. Sprinkle the gelatin over and set aside to soften.

Brown the hazelnuts in a nonstick skillet; set aside to cool.

Set the milk, Cognac and gelatin mixture over low heat and stir until the gelatin dissolves. Stir the breadcrumbs in for 2 minutes over low heat, to make a smooth paste. Remove from the heat.

Cut the duck breast into ½ inch (1 cm) slices. Season with salt and pepper. Set aside.

Cut the chicken breast and ham into cubes and put them into the food processor. Add the bread paste, salt, allspice and additional pepper to taste. Process on high speed for 30 seconds.

Add the garlic, shallots and egg to the processor and mix again for 30 seconds. Transfer the mixture to a large bowl; stir in the hazelnuts.

Oil a 20 fl oz (500 ml) ceramic terrine and coat it with a thin layer of the processed mixture. Cover with slices of duck. Continue layering in this manner, finishing with a layer of the hazelnut mixture. Press down well. Brush the surface with oil and cover the terrine. Bake in the preheated oven for 1¾ hours.

Let the terrine cool before refrigerating for at least 12 hours before serving.

Serve at room temperature, sliced and accompanied by gherkins, onions and cherries in vinegar, toast and a salad in season.

RABBIT TERRINE WITH PISTACHIO NUTS

Terrine de lapereau aux pistaches   Serves 6

Some families in France have secret recipes for preparing this kind of terrine, which have been handed down from generation to generation. In the past, the mistress of the house might have spent two or three days at a stretch preparing a small masterpiece like this, to be served on feast days or special occasions.

1 loin and 2 back legs of a young rabbit (about 1¼ lb/600 g), cut into serving pieces

1 onion, sliced

1 carrot, sliced

1 garlic clove, peeled but left whole

1 teaspoon coarse sea salt

6 green peppercorns

1 thyme sprig

1 bay leaf

2 parsley sprigs

2 whole cloves

½ teaspoon coriander seeds

⅓ cup (3 fl oz/90 ml) dry white wine

1¾ oz (50 g) dried currants

3 tablespoons muscat

2 oz (60 g) shelled and skinned pistachio nuts

1 sachet madeira jelly powder (or 2 tablespoons madeira and 1 teaspoon/5 g powdered — 2 leaves — unflavored gelatin)

1 tablespoon pink peppercorns

2 teaspoons (10 g) powdered (4 leaves) unflavored gelatin

4 pinches grated nutmeg

Put the rabbit, onion, carrot and garlic into a casserole. Add the salt, green peppercorns, thyme, bay leaf, parsley, cloves and coriander seeds. Pour in the white wine and 2 cups (16 fl oz/500 ml) cold water. Bring to a boil and cook, skimming, for 5 minutes. Cover and cook for 1 hour, until the rabbit meat is very tender and comes away from the bones.

Meanwhile, put the currants in a small nonaluminum saucepan. Pour in the muscat, bring to a boil and remove from the heat. Toast the pistachios over low heat in a nonstick skillet.

Make up the madeira jelly with 1⅔ cups (13 fl oz/410 ml) water (or make up the gelatin and add Madeira), and let it cool. Pour it into a 4 cup (1 qt/1 l) glass or ceramic terrine and turn the terrine so the jelly runs over the bottom and the sides. Crush the pink peppercorns between your fingers and scatter them over the jelly. Pour over a second layer of jelly.

When the meat is cooked, lift it out of the pot with tongs. Pull the meat off the bones. Strain the cooking liquid. Boil over high heat until reduced to 1 cup (8 fl oz/250 ml).

In a small nonaluminum saucepan, sprinkle the gelatin over 2 tablespoons of cold water and set aside to soften. When softened, set the mixture over low heat until the gelatin dissolves. Add to the reduced hot broth (stock). Stir and remove from the heat.

Put the meat in a food processor and add the broth and gelatin mixture. Process to a mousse-like texture. Add the nutmeg and mix again.

Spread a quarter of this mixture on the jelly coating in the terrine and scatter half the pistachios over it. Cover with a second layer of mousse and scatter with currants. Add a third layer of mousse and the remaining pistachios, and finish with a layer of the mousse, smoothing the surface with a spatula. Pour a thin layer of madeira jelly over the top. Cover and put the terrine in the refrigerator to chill for 8 hours before serving.

Serve sliced and accompanied with salad and raw vegetables.

Fish platter with Chinoiserie design, made in the Lunéville porcelain factory which operated from 1766–*circa* 1777; MUSEE NATIONAL DE CERAMIQUE, SEVRES
Soft-paste porcelain was made in the factory until the advent of hard-paste in 1770.

STUFFED CABBAGE TERRINE

Chou farci en terrine   Serves 6

A specialty of Central France, stuffed cabbage is a substantial and quite remarkable dish. A true stuffed cabbage is a meal in itself. This recipe shows well how our contemporary cuisine adapts and creates variations on old themes to create a lighter version of the age-old tradition.

Rabbit terrine with pistachio nuts (left); Stuffed cabbage terrine (right)

2 small legs or 6 thigh pieces of preserved duck
  (duck confit), with fat

4 onions, finely diced

4 carrots, finely diced

2 celery ribs (stalks), finely diced

2 shallots, finely diced

4 thyme sprigs

4 bay leaves

2 garlic cloves, crushed

10 oz (315 g) smoked bacon, finely chopped

14 oz (440 g) ham, minced

3 cups (6½ oz/200 g) fresh breadcrumbs

4 tablespoons minced parsley

48 juniper berries, bruised

4 eggs

salt and freshly ground pepper

16 leaves of curly green cabbage

Melt 4 tablespoons of the duck fat in a sauté pan. Add the diced vegetables, thyme and bay leaves and cook for about 5 minutes, until lightly browned. Add the garlic and the bacon. Brown for a few minutes and take the pan off the heat. Remove the thyme sprigs and bay leaves. Add the ham, breadcrumbs, parsley and juniper berries and mix.

Remove the skin and bones from the duck and tease out the meat with a fork: you should have

about 13 oz (410 g). Add the meat to the sauté pan and mix.

Break the eggs into a bowl. Season with salt and pepper and beat with a fork. Pour into the sauté pan and mix well.

In a large stockpot blanch the cabbage leaves in boiling water for 6 minutes. Drain them and drop them straight into cold water. Dry on a cloth and remove the tough ribs.

Select an 11 inch (28 cm) cast-iron or ceramic terrine with a lid. Coat the inside with some of the duck fat. Line the base with 2 leaves of cabbage cut in two and the sides with 6 leaves, letting them overhang the rim of the terrine. Fill with half of the stuffing. Cover with 4 cabbage leaves cut in two. Add the remaining stuffing and fold the leaves lining the sides over the top of the filling. Brush the surface with duck fat and put the lid on the terrine.

Bring some water to a boil in a fish poacher or other large pot. Place the terrine on a rack and cover the pot. Steam for 1 hour. Remove the terrine and unmold the stuffed cabbage onto a plate. Garnish with tarragon leaves. Slice and serve hot, with Celeriac Snowball (p. 191).

Eggs mimosa with tuna mousse (left); Scrambled eggs with salmon roe (right)

EGGS MIMOSA WITH TUNA MOUSSE

Oeufs mimosa à la mousse de thon   Serves 6

Eggs mimosa, like celeriac *rémoulade*, has appeared as part of the display of Sunday *hors d'oeuvres* on almost every French table. This recipe gives them refinement and subtlety, demonstrating perfectly the flexibility of some of the basic recipes in the French repertoire.

9 hardboiled eggs

3½ oz (100 g) tuna packed in olive oil, drained
and 1 tablespoon of the oil reserved

¼ cup (2 fl oz/60 ml) thick crème fraîche

1 tablespoon drained capers

1 teaspoon anchovy paste

1 tablespoon dark rum or Cognac

½ teaspoon curry powder

grated zest (rind) of 1 lemon or lime

salt and freshly ground pepper

Shell the eggs and halve them lengthwise. Set aside the yolks of 4 eggs for the mimosa and put the other yolks in the bowl of a food processor. Add the tuna, *crème fraîche*, capers, anchovy paste, the reserved oil, rum, curry powder, citrus zest and salt and pepper to taste. Process for 1 minute, until the mixture has a creamy consistency. It should not be too thin.

Fill the eggwhite halves with the tuna cream, returning them to their original shape. Arrange them on a large round platter.

Grate the reserved egg yolks over the stuffed eggs to cover with the mimosa. Keep in a cool place until ready to serve.

Serve with lettuce leaves, tomato slices and black olives.

Note: These eggs may be prepared several hours ahead; it can only improve them.

SCRAMBLED EGGS WITH SALMON ROE

Oeufs brouillés aux oeufs de saumon   Serves 4

Whether scrambled, in omelets or in soufflés, and varied with every imaginable sauce, eggs have always been part of the French appetizer selection, from the Middle Ages to the present. Today, however, this type of dish would be just as suited to the place of honor in a light luncheon.

8 eggs
salt and freshly ground pepper
2 tablespoons (1 oz/30 g) butter
¼ cup (2 fl oz/60 ml) thick crème fraîche
1 tablespoon minced chives
2 oz (60 g) salmon caviar (roe)
4 small dill sprigs

Break the eggs into a bowl and beat them with a fork, adding some salt and pepper.

Melt the butter in a small saucepan over very low heat. Add the beaten eggs through a strainer (this will give you a smooth mixture and eliminate the threads). Cook the eggs over very low heat, whisking all the while, until you have a thick,

Civet of eggs

smooth cream. Cooking time will vary according to taste, but the eggs must on no account become hard or crumbly — they must remain creamy.

Take the saucepan off the heat and pour in the *crème fraîche*; this will stop the cooking and make the eggs even creamier. Add the chives and mix.

Divide the eggs among 4 deep plates, garnish with salmon roe and dill and serve. These eggs may be eaten warm or cold.

CIVET OF EGGS

Civet d'oeufs   Serves 2

This fourteenth-century recipe is taken from the *Ménagier de Paris*, where it appears as *civés d'oeufs* ("stewed" eggs). The vinegar and wine sauce is curiously reminiscent of another Burgundian regional dish, the *meurette*, and also of *oeufs en matelote* (eggs in red wine sauce). The eggs are poached rather than fried in their dishes, but the tradition is the same.

> Poach your eggs in oil, then have some cooked onions cut into rings, and fry them in oil, then add wine, verjuice and vinegar and bring to the boil, and boil them all together; then in each bowl put three or four eggs, and over these pour the liquid, and this is not to be thickened.

2 tablespoons vegetable oil
3 onions (about 8 oz/250 g), thinly sliced
4 pinches sugar
1 tablespoon balsamic vinegar or aged wine
  vinegar
1 teaspoon sherry vinegar
3 tablespoons dry red wine
salt and freshly ground pepper
4 small eggs

Heat the oil in a large nonstick sauté pan. Add the onions and brown, stirring, over high heat. Lower the heat and simmer for 12 minutes. Add 2 tablespoons of water and the sugar and cook for 3 minutes more.

Add the vinegars and cook until they evaporate. Add the wine and salt and pepper to taste. Break the eggs, one by one, into a cup and add them individually to the sauté pan. Cook for 1 minute and remove from the heat.

Divide the egg ragoût between 2 plates and serve immediately, with toast.

Bacon and onion quiche

BACON AND ONION QUICHE

Quiche au lard à l'oignon   Serves 6

The true quiche is the one from Lorraine, a French provincial specialty that has conquered both the international gastronomic world and the food production industry: if there is one French dish known everywhere in the world it is the quiche. The classic recipe uses only bacon, eggs, and cream. Here the addition of onions makes it even tastier.

1 cup (3½ oz/100 g) all-purpose (plain) flour
4 pinches salt
¼ cup (2 oz/60 g) butter, softened
3 eggs
1 tablespoon peanut oil
5 oz (155 g) smoked bacon, thinly sliced
2 tablespoons (1 oz/30 g) butter
1 medium onion, sliced
1½ oz (45 g) Gruyère cheese, grated
¾ cup (6½ fl oz/200 ml) light (single) cream
salt and freshly ground pepper
⅓ teaspoon grated nutmeg

Make the pastry. Mound the flour on a work surface, sprinkle the salt over it and make a well in the center. Cut the butter into small pieces and put them in the well with 1 egg. Mix with the tips of the fingers, from the center outwards, working quickly and not kneading the dough too much. As soon as it no longer sticks to your fingers, roll it into a ball and put it in a plastic bag. Refrigerate for 15 minutes.

Roll out the dough on a work surface. Butter a 10¼ inch (26 cm) tart pan and line it with the dough. Prick several times with a fork, without piercing the dough right through; refrigerate for 25 minutes, or until firm.

Meanwhile, prepare the filling. Heat the oil in a 9½ inch (24 cm) nonstick skillet and brown the bacon strips quickly. Remove and set aside on a plate. Wipe out the pan and melt the butter in it. Add the onion and quickly brown. Set aside on a second plate.

Preheat the oven to 450°F (230°C/Gas 8). Take the pastry shell from the refrigerator and cover it with the onions. Scatter the bacon strips over the top and sprinkle with the grated cheese.

Pour the cream into a saucepan and bring just to a simmer.

Break the remaining 2 eggs into a ceramic or glass bowl and beat them with a fork. Gradually beat in the hot cream, salt, pepper and nutmeg. Carefully pour this mixture into the tart shell.

Bake for about 45 minutes, until golden. Remove from the oven and let rest for 10 minutes before serving it warm.

Meal in the country, an illuminated page from a Latin Bible from the Abbaye St Amand (1526–1559);
BIBLIOTHEQUE MUNICIPALE, VALENCIENNES

Roquefort puffs (left); Eggs with truffle cream (right, see p. 70)

ROQUEFORT PUFFS

Feuilleté au roquefort   Serves 4

Roquefort is without doubt one of the oldest of French cheeses. It has been known since the eleventh century, and it is even possible that it was made as early as the Gallo-Roman era. Made with ewe's milk and ripened for long periods in the airy natural vaults of the Larzac plateau, it is for many French people the king of cheeses. This recipe, in which it is cooked in a fine puff pastry, is somewhat reminiscent of the little tartlets of medieval times, made with fresh cheese, known as *talmouses*.

6½ oz (200 g) puff pastry
8 walnut halves
2¾ oz (80 g) Roquefort cheese, at room temperature
2¾ oz (80 g) cream cheese, at room temperature
½ teaspoon Cognac
salt and freshly ground pepper
⅓ cup (3 fl oz/90 ml) light (single) cream
nutmeg, grated

Preheat the oven to 450°F (230°C/Gas 8). Roll out the pastry ⅛ inch (3 mm) thick and cut it into 12 rectangles, each 4 x 2¼ inches (10 x 6 cm). Prick each rectangle so it will not puff up too much during cooking. Place the pastry on a moistened nonstick baking sheet. Bake for 12 to 15 minutes, until golden.

While the pastry is cooking, prepare the Roquefort filling. Coarsely grate the walnuts. Mash the Roquefort with a fork in a deep plate and incorporate the cream cheese, the walnuts, and the Cognac. Season with salt and pepper. Whip the cream until it is thick and adheres to the wires of the whisk. Fold it into the cheese mixture.

Assemble the puffs: place a pastry square on a baking sheet and spread with the Roquefort filling. Place a second square on top, add another layer of filling, and place a third pastry square on top. Proceed with layering and filling to make 3 more filled pastries. Sprinkle the top of the pastry with grated nutmeg. Heat in the hot oven for 3 minutes.

Serve at once, accompanied with a lamb's lettuce salad (corn salad) and cubes of raw apple and beet (beetroot), dressed with sherry vinegar and walnut oil.

Thread-patterned silverware, Charles Christofle (1805–63);
MUSEE CONDE, CHANTILLY

EGGS WITH TRUFFLE CREAM

Oeufs cocotte à la crème de truffe Serves 4

Eggs and truffles are truly made for each other! The truffle omelet has always been the principal specialty of the regions where truffles are found, such as Périgord, Drome, and Haute Provence. This wonderful plant, glittering like a black diamond, lends an incomparable flavor to the foods with which it is served and has been a star component of French cuisine for 300 years. Its rarity and exorbitant price have made it a symbol of the most lavish gastronomy.

1 fresh or dried truffle (about 2 oz/60 g)
2 tablespoons Fine Champagne Cognac
¾ cup (6½ fl oz/200 ml) light (single) cream
2 pinches grated nutmeg
2 pinches salt
4 pinches ground white pepper
4 eggs

Put a rack in the bottom of a large saucepan. Set 4 buttered 4 inch (10 cm) ceramic or earthenware ramekins on it. Pour water into the pan to reach to ½ inch (1 cm) below the rims of the ramekins, holding them down on the rack with the palm of your hand to prevent them floating. Remove the ramekins from the saucepan and heat the water to a simmer.

Brush the truffle clean under running water and peel it (keep the skin to flavor stuffing or salad oil). Cut it in quarters and coarsely grate it.

Pour the Cognac into a small saucepan and set over low heat. Ignite it, and when the flame goes out add the cream, nutmeg, salt and pepper. Boil for 3 minutes, until the cream coats the back of a spoon. Add the grated truffle, mix for 5 seconds and remove from the heat.

Put a spoonful of the truffle cream into each ramekin and break an egg into each. Place the ramekins on the rack in the water, which must be barely simmering. Cover and cook for 7 minutes.

Place each ramekin on a plate with a folded napkin or a doily beneath it. Serve at once, with buttered toast. (See photograph p. 69.)

ARTICHOKE SALAD WITH FOIE GRAS

Salade d'artichauts au foie gras Serves 4

Queen Catherine de' Medici, it is said, almost died of indigestion caused by artichokes, of which she was inordinately fond. This edible flower, which has long been popular in the South of France, became fashionable and made its official début in the kitchen at the time of the Renaissance, due to Italian influence. Brittany produces a beautiful large variety known as the macau, while the ones grown in the Midi are a finer, smaller purple variety, some of them so tender they can be eaten raw.

4 artichokes (about 10 oz/315 g each)
½ lemon
4 shallots, minced
1½ tablespoons balsamic vinegar
salt and freshly ground pepper
¼ cup (2¾ fl oz/80 ml) peanut (groundnut) oil
1 small head lamb's lettuce (corn salad), or 1
   small head Boston lettuce (about 4 oz/125 g)
4 slices foie gras (preserved goose liver)

Break off the artichoke stalks level with the hearts. Discard the tough leaves, and cut off the tips of the inner leaves ½ inch (1 cm) from the hearts. Trim the hearts and rub with the lemon. Drop the hearts into a saucepan of boiling water, add the juice of the half lemon and cook for about 20 minutes, until very tender.

In a bowl, combine the shallots, vinegar and salt and pepper. Add the oil, whisking it in with a fork.

When the artichokes are cooked, drain them and put one in the center of each plate. Take the shallots out of the vinaigrette and divide them among the artichoke hearts.

Put the lettuce in a salad bowl and dress with the vinaigrette. Distribute the salad around the artichokes. Place a slice of *foie gras* on each artichoke. Serve immediately, accompanied with toasted *brioches*. Add pepper before eating.
Note: The liver slices may be garnished with a small amount of minced truffle.

Artichoke salad with foie gras

Smoked salmon rillettes (top); Bell pepper bavarois with tomato coulis (bottom)

SMOKED SALMON RILLETTES

Rillettes de saumon fumé   Serves 6

Originally, *rillettes* were made at the time the annual pig was slaughtered for salting and preparing the meat supply for the ensuing twelve months. Pieces of the meat are cooked in lard for a long time to form a sort of creamy salted pâté which keeps for long periods and is eaten on bread. *Rillettes* are also made with goose meat. This recipe is a fine example of modern culinary creativity, starting from a traditional dish and transforming the ingredients into an innovative and exquisite delicacy.

1 teaspoon (5 g) powdered (2 leaves) unflavored gelatin

⅓ cup (3 fl oz/90 ml) light (single) cream

1 lb (500 g) smoked salmon

grated zest (rind) and juice of 1 lemon

1 teaspoon finely and freshly ground pepper

3 pinches powdered cayenne pepper

2 tablespoons minced chives

1 tablespoon extra virgin olive oil

Sprinkle the gelatin over 1 tablespoon of the cream in a small saucepan. Heat gently until the gelatin melts, then remove from the heat and add the rest of the cream. Set aside to cool.

Cut half the salmon into pieces and put it into the bowl of a food processor with the cooled cream. Mix thoroughly. Add the lemon zest, pepper, cayenne and chives, and process for 10 seconds.

Put 1 tablespoon of the lemon juice in a large bowl and mix in the oil. Roughly chop the remaining salmon and add it to the lemon mixture. Gradually stir in the salmon cream. Transfer the mixture to a terrine, cover, and refrigerate. The *rillettes* may be prepared 24 hours in advance.

Serve with a garnish of dill and quarters of lemon, scallions (spring onions), cucumber, etc.

BELL PEPPER BAVAROIS WITH TOMATO COULIS

Bavarois de poivron au coulis de tomate   Serves 4

The *bavarois*, or Bavarian cream, is a kind of custard in which gelatin is used as a setting agent. It was very popular during the last century, both as a sweet side-dish and as a dessert. Using vegetables, Nouvelle Cuisine expanded this theme to produce savory versions, of which this recipe with its southern accents is a good example.

4 large red bell peppers (capsiums) (about 6½ oz/ 200 g each)
salt and freshly ground pepper
4 pinches powdered cumin
4 pinches hot paprika
6 pinches sweet paprika
2 teaspoons (10 g) powdered (4 leaves) unflavored gelatin
⅓ cup (3 fl oz/90 ml) light (single) cream
1 teaspoon oil
1¼ lb (600 g) ripe tomatoes
2 teaspoons wine vinegar
⅓ cup (3 fl oz/90 ml) extra virgin olive oil
4 basil sprigs

Grill the bell peppers under the broiler (grill) or over charcoal on a barbecue, until they are brown all over, but not charred. The cooking takes about 30 minutes. Put the peppers in a covered casserole and let cool for 15 to 20 minutes. Peel the peppers, split them in half and reserve the juice that runs out; discard the stalk, seeds and white filaments.

Cut the peppers lengthwise into ½ inch (1 cm) strips. Set aside 12 of the strips; put the others in

Manda Lamétrie, the farmer's wife, Alfred Roll (1846–1919);
MUSEE D'ORSAY, PARIS
Curdled milk was once used in many country recipes; *lait cuit* is left to curdle and then heated. It is eaten with buckwheat pancakes.

a food processor with the reserved juice, salt, pepper, cumin and paprikas. Process to a very smooth purée, and transfer to a bowl.

Soak the gelatin leaves in cold water to soften, then drain and put them in a small saucepan. Melt, stirring, over gentle heat. Pour this gelatin in a thin stream into the purée, whisking all the time. Refrigerate until the mixture begins to set.

Whip the cream until it forms peaks between the wires of the whisk. Whisk it into the half-set pepper purée.

Using a pastry brush, oil 4 ramekins. Line the bases and sides with the reserved pepper strips and pour the purée into the center. Fold the pepper strips over the top. Cover and refrigerate for at least 6 hours.

Prepare the coulis. Plunge the tomatoes into boiling water for 10 seconds, refresh under running water and then peel, halve and remove the seeds. Coarsely chop the flesh and put it into a food processor with the vinegar, oil and salt and pepper. Process on high speed for 2 minutes, until the mixture is very smooth and coral in color. Cover and refrigerate.

At serving time, unmold each *bavarois* onto the center of a plate. Surround it with the tomato coulis and decorate with basil sprigs.

Still life with oysters, Osias Beert the Elder (1570–1624); MUSEES ROYAUX DES BEAUX-ARTS, BRUSSELS Guy de Maupassant wrote of one variety of oyster that they melted "between th

late and the tongue like salted sweets."

SEAFOOD

Mussels and oysters, various shellfish, cuttlefish and squid, lobsters and crayfish, shrimp, prawns, and scampi, not to mention frogs and snails, appear only rarely in the recipe collections of the medieval period. Naturally, those who lived close to the sea or who had access to streams and rivers were more likely to have taken advantage of them. In a town such as Paris, far from the coast, shellfish were a luxury. In *Le Ménagier de Paris* only oysters are mentioned, and they were eaten cooked, either grilled or fried. Mussels were a plebeian food, good for peasants and fishermen. According to the recipes they were prepared *à la marinière*, cooked quickly in a pot with very little water, over high heat. They were seasoned with vinegar. Other recipes prepare them as a soup, with verjuice and parsley root. But this was not *grande cuisine*. Snails and frogs feature here and there, as a common food but nevertheless appreciated by some individuals. As for crustaceans they are simply not mentioned. Only with the sixteenth and seventeenth centuries did crustaceans and shellfish finally assume their due role in the cuisine of the wealthy.

In a text written at the end of the seventeenth century oysters are referred to as "sea creatures which feed themselves from between two shells; they are highly prized by epicures and are eaten while still alive."

The Romans were the first to farm oysters in special areas of the Adriatic coast and then also along areas of the Mediterranean and on some parts of the coast of southern France such as Leucate, near Perpignan. After the fall of their Empire, all was lost, sites and techniques. Only the natural oyster beds of the seas were left. These were considered adequate for many centuries as they managed to assuage the appetite of coastal inhabitants, and some gourmets in a few towns. When the demand became too great, then the natural oyster beds became depleted. When importing them from other countries became too costly some ingenious individuals applied themselves to reviving the old Roman techniques of oyster farming with great success, first in Brittany, then further along the coast towards Bordeaux and Arcachon, and then in Normandy. In France today, several varieties of oysters are commonly raised on special oyster beds which stretch for miles along some parts of the coast.

The round flat oysters, called *belons*, after the river mouth they originate from, are the most rare and expensive. Their taste is nutty, sweet, and very subtle. The *marennes,*

A luncheon of oysters, Jean-François de Troy (1679–1752); MUSEE CONDE, CHANTILLY
Apart from savoring oysters in their raw state, the renowned chef François Massialot suggested cooking them and gave recipes for duck with oysters, and an oyster and truffle sauce in his *Cuisinier Royal et Bourgeois* of 1691.

Still life with lobster (detail),
Anne Vallayer-Coster (1744–1818);
THE LOUVRE, PARIS
The curious appearance of this crustacean
alarmed the Princess de Lamballe
(director of the household of Marie-
Antoinette) to such a degree that it was
reported "she closed her eyes and
remained motionless for half an hour."

hollower, and light green in color, are more common, but have an even finer taste — when
you eat them raw, you absorb the very essence of the sea.

To transport these shellfish was very expensive, and it was only the aristocrats and
the wealthy who could afford them. And in such quantities! It is said that Henri IV ate as
many as 300 oysters at dinner. Louis XVIII, having taken refuge at Ghent, finished his meal
by eating a good hundred of them. In the course of particularly pantagruelian feasts, the
writer Crebillon the Younger managed to consume a hundred dozen oysters! In the sixteenth century no-one cared how they were eaten, raw or cooked, roast or boiled and
marinated. As time went on, more often they were preferred raw. But Vincent de la
Chapelle, one of the greats of cuisine during the following century, suggested a dish of

pheasant with oysters, and in the eighteenth century the esteemed Marin recommended an omelet made with a dozen eggs and three dozen oysters — and that for one person! Men were particularly crazy about oysters because of their reputation of being an aphrodisiac. Casanova and many other eighteenth-century writers raved about their essential role in dinners where the main intent was seduction. Things calmed down somewhat in the nineteenth century, and gradually oyster consumption settled at the decidedly more reasonable level of contemporary society.

Crayfish, both fresh and saltwater, and lobsters had an important place on tables from the eighteenth century. At this time, lobsters were still called *écrevisses de mer*. They were far from being the principal constituent of a dish but rather were just another element in its composition or a garnish. It was the same for shrimp and prawns. In Paris, crustaceans featured only on the tables of the rich, and the same went for all other kinds of fresh seafood. Lobsters and crayfish thus acquired their reputation, which they have kept to this day, of being delicate special-occasion foods. In the nineteenth century, together with truffles, they came to symbolize if not good living then at least a luxury cuisine and often were snobbishly more appreciated for their price than for their flavor.

Crabs, shrimp, prawns, cuttlefish, and squid have until recently remained strictly regional foods, adding to the exotic flavor of coastal cuisines. As for frogs and snails, which for Anglo-Saxons have always represented, and still do, the foreignness of French cooking, they have had one of the most modest places on noble tables, for they belong primarily

Still life, Théodule Ribot (1823–91); MUSEE DES BEAUX-ARTS, CAEN
The Ancient Greeks not only loved to eat oysters, they also used the shells for casting votes. The voter inscribed his preference on the white mother-of-pearl.

Still life with crayfish, Sébastian Stosskopf (1596/7–1657); MUSEE DES BEAUX-ARTS, LE HAVRE
Crayfish were extremely cheap in Paris in the 1630s and were consumed in large quantities. By the turn of the century, they had increased from three francs per hundred to forty francs, and consumption dropped accordingly. But the price gave them a certain cachet among the rich and they became synonymous with luxury and decadence.

to peasant and provincial traditions. Among these of course, the *escargots de Bourgogne* are the best example of how humble country fare can in time become a delicious, garlic-scented and buttery dish epitomizing the French provincial traditions!

The sumptuous seafood platters of oysters, mussels, cockles, clams, prawns, shrimp, and crabs, typical of Parisian brasseries, offer the merest glimpse of the shellfish and crustacean treasures from the Atlantic and Mediterranean coasts. Towards the north, from the Pas de Calais and Normandy to Brittany and further, to the Saintonge, the most common and most popular shellfish are mussels. The usual style of preparation is *à la marinière*, cooked with a little white wine, onions, and parsley, but in the region of the Charente this gives way to the magnificent *mouclade*, in which the mussels cook in a delicious saffron-flavored sauce made with cream and white wine. Farmed on wooden stakes planted on the sea floor, or gathered from the rocks at low tide, mussels have been the food of fishermen for a long time. The tiny prawns known as *crevettes grises* are also exquisite; they are caught along sandy beaches with large nets, known as *pousseux*, quickly cooked in boiling water and eaten with brown bread and fresh butter. Clams and cockles may be eaten either raw or cooked and are often "stuffed" — in other words, baked with a garlic- and parlsey-flavored butter. From the Atlantic also comes the scallop, queen of shellfish and star of seafood cuisine: each of the great cooks of our time has created

Still life with lobster, Eugène Delacroix (1798–1863); THE LOUVRE, PARIS
Delacroix was greatly interested in English art and in animal painting, and was an admirer of Constable. Although perhaps best known for his large-scale decorations for civic buildings, Delacroix found his smaller, freely handled, colorful compositions featuring battles, hunts, and animals in combat the more satisfying.

Lunch in the studio, Edouard Manet (1832–83); BAYERISCHE STAATSGALERIE, MUNICH Manet imbued his works with a great sense of immediacy through his practice of painting from the model. He frequently favored a restricted palette in which black was extremely prominent.

an elegant recipe for this ingredient. The large and handsome crabs known as *tourteaux*, boiled then cooled, are traditionally served as they are, accompanied by mayonnaise and a nutcracker to crack the hard shells of the legs and claws. Spider crabs, with a more delicate flesh, are cooked very quickly and served in the same way. Decidedly more rare are lobsters, and when they are not served with a lemony mayonnaise, they are treated according to the precepts of *haute cuisine*. Winkles and *bulots* are offered as cocktail tidbits with apéritifs. Finally, and not to be forgotten, is the tasty *soupe aux étrilles* made with small swimmer crabs from the coasts of Normandy and Brittany, whose flavor is both powerful and subtle.

Besides the classic oysters, clams, and mussels, the Mediterranean shore offers some more unusual shellfish: the minuscule *tellines*, or wedge-shells, which, cooked with parsley, garlic, and white wine, make a finger-licking delicacy; the *violets de mer*, strange marine creatures whose shape and appearance are vaguely reminiscent of a potato and whose bright yellow flesh has a strong iodine flavor; octopus, lengthily cooked to make it tender; the *clovisses*, or clams; and the crayfish, finer-flavored than lobsters but today sadly disappearing from French Mediterranean waters as a result of overfishing. Cuttlefish and squid are a regional specialty along the Languedoc coast; they are cooked with garlic, tomato and saffron, with a hint of chili. At the other end of the Pyrénées, on the Basque coast, people prefer them cooked in their own ink.

Since the beginning of this century, seafood has gradually become more common. Thanks to rapid transport and new preservation techniques, they can now be found throughout the whole country, and they have become increasingly important in cuisine. Having at last left the dark recesses of regional curiosities, they have become indispensable prime ingredients for culinary creativity.

Creamed scallops (left); Scallops with boletus mushrooms (right)

CREAMED SCALLOPS

Coquilles Saint Jacques à la crème   Serves 2

Cooking with cream was for a long time typical of Normandy, a dairy-produce province if ever there was one. Then classical cuisine began to make extensive use of it and gave all dishes based on cream the title *à la normande*. Cream is often used in shellfish and other fish dishes, to which it gives a special, thick velvety texture. In this recipe it simply serves to bind a delicious saffron-flavored sauce.

12 large sea scallops with their roe* or 16 large sea scallops

2 shallots, minced

2 tablespoons dry white vermouth

6 tablespoons thick crème fraîche

1 teaspoon freshly ground black pepper

1 tablespoon lemon juice

4 pinches saffron threads

2 small tomatoes (6 oz/185 g), peeled, seeded and diced

24 tarragon leaves

¼ cup (2 oz/60 g) butter

Separate the scallops from their roe. Halve the white parts; set aside.

In an 8½ inch (22 cm) nonstick sauté pan, combine the shallot and vermouth. Place over medium heat and cook until all of the liquid evaporates. Add the *crème fraîche*, pepper, lemon juice and saffron and bring to a boil. Add the tomato and tarragon and mix. Add the scallop roe and cook for 1 minute. Add the white parts and cook, stirring, for 1 minute.

Divide the scallops between 2 warmed plates and serve immediately, accompanied with steamed diced cucumber and wild or brown rice.
Note: Scallops are sold without their roe in the United States.

SCALLOPS WITH BOLETUS MUSHROOMS

Coquilles Saint Jacques aux cèpes   Serves 2

In medieval times the scallop was the emblem of all pilgrims who undertook the pilgrimage of Saint Jacques de Compostelle. But it is also a succulent shellfish that is better eaten in winter. Its slightly sweet taste marries wonderfully well here with the flavor of the mushrooms.

12 large sea scallops with their roe or 16 large
   sea scallops*

12 small cèpes *(boletus) mushrooms, trimmed*

2 tablespoons extra virgin olive oil

¼ cup (2 oz/60 g) butter

2 shallots, minced

salt and freshly ground pepper

herbs for garnish

Separate the roe from the white part of the scallops. Slice each scallop crosswise into 3 rounds.
Cut the roe into ¼ inch (5 mm) strips.

Beginning with the rounded part of each cap,
thinly slice the mushrooms into disks, discarding
the last third of the stalk.

Heat the oil in a 9½ inch (24 cm) nonstick skillet. Add half the butter and the shallot and stir for
30 seconds over low heat. Add the mushroom
disks and cook for 1 minute over high heat, stirring all of the time. Add salt to taste. Lift the
mushrooms and shallot out of the pan with a slotted spoon and divide between 2 warmed plates.

Add the roe to the skillet and stir-fry for 30
seconds. Add the scallops and stir-fry for 30
seconds. Season with salt. Lift them out of the pan
with a slotted spoon and add to the mushrooms.

Over high heat reduce the cooking juices that
remain in the pan. Stir in the remaining 1 tablespoon of butter until melted.

Coat the scallops with the sauce and serve with
a purée of potatoes cooked with oil and cream and
garnish with herbs. Add pepper just before eating.
*Note: Scallops are sold without their roe in the
United States.

*Fish shop and laundry women's boat at the Quay of the Mégisserie
(*circa* 1670);* MUSEE CARNAVALET, PARIS

Scallops and langoustines in sea salt

SCALLOPS AND LANGOUSTINES IN SEA SALT

*Coquilles Saint Jacques et langoustines
au gros sel*
                    Serves 3

I n its perfect simplicity this dish transports us straight to the
Atlantic coasts of Brittany and Normandy. Here the fisherfolk
take the sea's produce and cook it as it is, without embellishment
and absolutely fresh, its perfect taste unspoilt.

*9 langoustines (Dublin Bay prawns or scampi),
   king prawns, yabbies or jumbo shrimp*

9 sea scallops, roe removed

3 tablespoons extra virgin olive oil

1 tablespoon freshly ground black pepper

1 teaspoon coarse sea salt

Shell the langoustines and devein them. Brush
the langoustines and scallops with 1 tablespoon of
the olive oil.

Sprinkle the pepper into an 8½ inch (22 cm)
nonstick sauté pan and place over low heat. Let
the pepper heat gently and then pour in the
remaining 2 tablespoons of oil. Add the
langoustines and scallops and cook over high heat
for 40 seconds on each side. Sprinkle with the sea
salt.

Divide the seafood among 3 warmed plates and
drizzle with the pan juices. Serve at once, accompanied with a salad of lamb's lettuce (corn salad)
very lightly dressed with aged wine vinegar.

SQUID WITH HAM STUFFING

Calmars farcis au jambon   Serves 4

Surely nature created squid to be stuffed! And French cooking, both local and classic, has always made extensive use of stuffings; hence this dish with its hint of Southern flavors.

8 small squid (about 3½ oz/100 g each)

2 slices (1½ oz/45 g) white sandwich bread, without crusts

2 garlic cloves

1½ oz (45 g) raw ham, chopped

1 egg

1 tablespoon minced flat-leaf (Italian) parsley

salt and freshly ground pepper

4 pinches grated nutmeg

2 tablespoons extra virgin olive oil

2 oz (60 g) very ripe cherry tomatoes, quartered

To prepare the squid, place the first one flat on a work surface and hold the tube in one hand. Take the tentacles in the other hand and pull gently. Discard the bone and intestines. From the head, keep only the tentacles cut off level with the eyes; wash them and wipe dry. Wash the inside of the squid, and if there are any eggs or roe leave them: they are excellent. Peel off the fine iridescent skin, and wipe the tube dry. Detach the wings and add them to the tentacles. Follow the same procedure with the remaining squid. Chop half the tentacles and wings.

Preheat the oven to 450°F (230°C/Gas 8). Reduce the bread to coarse crumbs in a blender or food processor. Brown the crumbs lightly in a dry nonstick skillet and pour into a bowl. Crush 1 clove of the garlic and add to the bowl. Beat egg, mix with ham and add to bread and garlic. Next add the parsley, salt and pepper to taste and the nutmeg.

Squid with ham stuffing (left); Parsleyed baby squid (right)

Heat ½ tablespoon of the oil in a 9½ inch (24 cm) nonstick skillet. Cook the tentacles over low heat for 3 minutes. Add the contents of the bowl and mix for 30 seconds. Sprinkle with ½ tablespoon of olive oil, mix again and remove from the heat. Set aside to cool.

Fill the squid mantles with the stuffing and secure with a toothpick. Wash the stuffed squid under running water, holding them pointed end up. Wipe dry.

Slice the remaining garlic clove. Pour the remaining 1 tablespoon of oil into a 12½ x 8½ inch (32 x 22 cm) ovenproof dish. Add the tomatoes, garlic and salt and pepper to taste; mix well. Lay the stuffed squid head-to-tail in the dish and turn them so that they are coated in the flavored oil. Bake for 15 minutes in the preheated oven. Baste the squid, turn them over and bake for 15 minutes longer.

Remove from the oven and arrange on a serving dish. Serve hot, warm or cold.

PARSLEYED BABY SQUID

Petits calmars sautés à la persillade   Serves 4

Traditionally the people of the Midi or the Basque coast would eat squid more readily than their compatriots further north. But in the past few years, thanks to a growing interest in the produce of the sea, these little cephalopods have gained ground and are now enjoyed at every table.

3 lb (1.5 kg) baby squid, cleaned
salt and freshly ground pepper
3 pinches grated nutmeg
3 tablespoons extra virgin olive oil
2 garlic cloves, minced
3 tablespoons minced flat-leaf (Italian) parsley

Separate the tube from the squid head by pulling it gently. The tube is emptied of the bone and the intestines except for the eggs and the soft roe which are very tasty. The only part of the head you need to keep are the tentacles. Cut each tube into rings 1 inch (2.5 cm) wide. Wash both tentacles and rings and wipe with care.

Put the squid into an 11 inch (28 cm) nonstick sauté pan and place over high heat. Cook, stirring constantly with a spatula, until the squid ceases to give off liquid and takes on a reddish brown tinge, after about 15 minutes.

When the squid pieces are cooked, add salt and pepper to taste, and the nutmeg, oil, garlic and parsley. Mix for 10 seconds and remove from the heat. Serve at once.

Note: If the squid are *very* small, the mantles may be left whole.

The falcon, Pierre Subleyras (1699–1749); THE LOUVRE, PARIS

Mussels in ramekins with walnut pistou (top); Mussels in curry cream (bottom)

MUSSELS IN CURRY CREAM

Moules à la crème au curry Serves 3–4

From the fourteenth century on, we find recipes for mussels that are practically identical to the classic *moules marinières*. These little shellfish abound along the Atlantic coast and in the English Channel. In the beginning mussels were food for the common fisher people, but little by little they gained status and made an appearance in the *grande cuisine*. This very refined dish has its roots in the famous *mouclade* of the Charente seaboard, with the curry in this case replacing the saffron and adding an exotic touch.

¾ cup (6½ fl oz/200 ml) dry white wine
2 shallots, minced
2 qt (2 l) cultivated mussels, scrubbed and debearded
1 tablespoon curry powder
½ cup (4 fl oz/125 ml) thick crème fraîche

Pour the wine into a large nonaluminum pan and add the shallots. Bring to a boil, and boil until the wine is reduced by half. Add the mussels and cook on high heat until they open, stirring 2 or 3 times. When all of the mussels are open, take them out with a skimmer and set aside in a large bowl.

Boil to reduce the cooking liquid by half. Add the curry powder and *crème fraîche*. Bring to a boil and simmer until thick and creamy. Strain into a bowl.

Return the mussels to the pan and coat them with the sauce. Reheat for a few minutes on high heat, turning the mussels as they heat.

Divide the mussels and sauce among 4 deep plates and serve immediately.

MUSSELS IN RAMEKINS WITH WALNUT PISTOU

Cassolettes de moules au pistou de noix Serves 4

Les moules de bouchot are cultivated mussels grown, as the name suggests, on *bouchots*, a kind of grille stretched between stakes set in the sea, where they attach themselves and proceed to fatten. All round the French coast, from the Etang de Thau on the Mediterranean through the Atlantic waters to the coastline of the English Channel, mussel farms proliferate.

This recipe, incorporating a variation of the Provençal *pistou*, demonstrates how deliciously one of the most widely consumed shellfish in France can be adapted to sauces of all kinds.

2 qt (2 l) cultivated mussels, scrubbed and debearded
1 small garlic clove
2 oz (60 g) shelled walnuts
2 tablespoons extra virgin olive oil
24 fresh basil leaves
freshly ground pepper

Wash the mussels and drain in a strainer; transfer them to a large pan. Cover, and let the mussels open over high heat, turning them 2 or 3 times. When all the mussels are open, take the pan from the heat and set aside to cool. Remove them from their shells and discard the shells. Put the mussels into an 8½ inch (22 cm) nonstick skillet.

Strain the liquid from the cooking pot — there will be about 1 cup (8 fl oz/250 ml) — into a small saucepan. Boil over high heat until reduced to ¼ cup (2 fl oz/60 ml) of syrupy liquid.

Prepare the walnut *pistou*. In a blender, combine the garlic, walnuts and olive oil. Add the basil leaves, pepper and 3 tablespoons of the reduced sauce from the mussels. Blend for 10 seconds, then taste. If the sauce is not too salty, add the rest of the liquid and blend for 10 seconds.

Pour the *pistou* over the mussels and heat very gently for 1 minute, without letting the sauce boil, otherwise the mussels will toughen and give off more liquid. Stir gently so that the mussels

Prawn and flower fritters

are well coated with sauce. Put the mussels and sauce into 4 ovenproof earthenware or ceramic ramekins and serve.

These mussels are eaten with a spoon, accompanied by toast. This very light appetizer can become a main dish if served in large bowls on a bed of buttered fresh noodles.

PRAWN AND FLOWER FRITTERS

Gambas et fleurs en beignets   Serves 6

Large prawns known as *gambas*, from the Continental shelf, are today consumed throughout France, and great French chefs have been devoting more and more attention to them. Here in the form of fritters, paired with the wonderful delicate flowers of zucchini (courgettes), they provide a good example of the search for refined simplicity that characterizes the contemporary *grande cuisine*.

24 uncooked large prawns or jumbo shrimp,
 2½–2¾ oz (75–80 g) each
6 zucchini (courgette) flowers
¾ cup (5½ fl oz/170 ml) ice water
1 egg yolk
1 cup (4 oz/125 g) all-purpose (plain) flour
4 pinches salt
3 cups (24 fl oz/750 ml) peanut (groundnut) oil
extra 2 tablespoons all-purpose (plain) flour

Cut off the prawn heads and peel the prawns, leaving the last joint of the shell and the tail intact. Pull out the thin black vein along the back. Make parallel shallow incisions along the underside so that the prawns will not curl up during cooking.

Remove the pistils from the zucchini flowers and cut the petals in two or three pieces according to size.

Make the fritter batter. In a bowl, combine the ice water and egg yolk and beat hard with a fork. Add the flour and some salt as you continue beating fast. The batter must be just bound, but not kneaded.

Heat the oil in a small deep-fryer or a deep saucepan. When it is hot enough (so that a piece of dough dropped in immediately surfaces), roll the prawns lightly in the flour, dip them in the batter and drop them into the oil. Cook for 3 minutes; lift out with a skimmer.

Dip the zucchini flowers in the batter. Drop them into the oil and cook for 1 minute only. Lift out the fritters with a skimmer and drain on paper towels. Transfer to a serving plate covered with a paper napkin and serve at once.

Note: This batter is suitable for making fritters of scallops, mussels, squares of cuttlefish, calamari rings, small pieces of salmon, sole or other fish, and all kinds of vegetables: zucchini, eggplant (aubergine), bell pepper (capsicum), carrot, cauliflower, etc.

Still life with seafood, Joseph Bail (1862–1921); ANCIENNE COLLECTION, BRAME AND LORENCEAU
Lobsters caught in cold waters, such as off the coast of Brittany, are considered the most flavorsome.

GRATIN OF OYSTERS

Huîtres gratinées   Serves 4

I n *La Maison Rustique*, published in the 1740s, much of which is devoted to technical advice on gardening, breeding and other subjects dear to the heart of farmers, we find a chapter containing a long series of recipes. This gratin features in it, and shows that even if the aristocrats and the wealthy liked to gorge themselves on raw oysters, there were some who enjoyed them just as much cooked.

> Take some oysters, open them and leave them in their own shells, put a little pepper, a little chopped parsley, a dab of butter and some very fine breadcrumbs on top; broil [grill] them and go over them with a red-hot salamander, and serve them at once.

24 large oysters
1 shallot, minced
¾ cup (6½ fl oz/200 ml) Champagne

⅓ cup (3 fl oz/90 ml) thick crème fraîche
2 pinches saffron threads
2 egg yolks
freshly ground pepper

Preheat the broiler (grill).

Shuck the oysters, reserving the deep shells and the oyster liquor. Strain the liquor.

In a nonaluminum sauté pan, combine the shallot and Champagne and bring to a boil. Boil for 30 seconds, then add the oysters and their liquor and cook for 10 seconds. Lift the oysters out with a skimmer and distribute them among the reserved shells.

Strain the cooking liquid into a small nonaluminum saucepan and reduce it to half over high heat. Stir in the *crème fraîche* and the saffron and reduce by one-third. Remove from the heat and whisk in the egg yolks. Season with pepper.

Coat the oysters with the sauce and arrange the shells on plates. Put the plates under the very hot broiler for 15 seconds, and serve at once.

OYSTERS IN MUSCAT

Huîtres au muscat de Beaumes de Venise   Serves 4

Oysters are always part of the fare for feast days and celebrations. They are an absolute must for midnight supper on Christmas Eve and New Year's Eve.

The French during the present century have preferred their oysters raw, and it took the revolution of Nouvelle Cuisine to convince them that cooked, as in this recipe, they are equally marvelous.

24 large oysters (flat yellow belons or green
  spéciales for preference)

1 shallot, minced

3 pinches freshly ground black pepper

⅔ cup (5 fl oz/155 ml) Beaumes de Venise muscat
  (see note below)

1 tablespoon finely snipped chives

⅓ cup (3 fl oz/90 ml) thick crème fraîche

2 tablespoons (1 oz/30 g) butter

Open the oysters and pull away the flat shells. Put the oysters into a strainer and let them drain over a bowl for 15 minutes.

Shuck the oysters, reserving their liquor. Strain all the liquor into a 9½ inch (24 cm) nonstick sauté pan. Add the shallot and pepper and bring to a boil. Add the wine and *crème fraîche* and as soon as it returns to a boil, put in the oysters. Simmer for 10 seconds, then turn over and simmer for another 5 seconds. Remove them with a skimmer and divide among 4 warmed plates.

Boil the sauce to reduce by half, and whisk in the butter. Strain the sauce over the oysters. Sprinkle on the chives and serve at once. Add pepper before eating. Accompany with wholemeal toast and sweet (unsalted) butter.

Note: The Beaumes de Venise muscat, an excellent liqueur wine, may be replaced by Rivesaltes muscat or by Sauternes.

Gratin of oysters (left); Oysters in muscat (right)

WARM OYSTER SALAD

Huîtres en salade tiède   Serves 4

On the French Atlantic and Mediterranean coasts the Romans invented oyster-breeding, which continued up to the time of the Barbarian invasions (between the fifth and seventh centuries). The Latin writer Ausone mentioned the oyster beds of Marseille, Port Vendres, the Médoc, Saintonge, and Calvados.

Whenever they are featured in recipe collections from the Middle Ages — most notably in Taillevent's *Le Viandier* and *Le Ménagier de Paris* — oysters are always cooked. They gained in popularity during the sixteenth and seventeenth centuries, and this led to a veritable "oystermania" in the eighteenth century.

The sixteenth-century satirist François Rabelais wrote of the Busch oysters from the Arcachon Basin as being the best. Rondelet, another writer, informs us that "those from Brittany are praised above all the rest; those from Bordeaux are judged to be the best after the ones from Brittany, among which those from the Médoc are much esteemed." Dinner guests consumed dozens of them at a time, and they acquired a reputation for being aphrodisiàcs when eaten raw, which has now become the classic way of eating them.

13 oz (410 g) firm-textured potatoes, peeled
16 large oysters
1 tablespoon aged wine vinegar
1 small fresh or dried truffle (about 1 oz/30 g)
3 tablespoons extra virgin olive oil
1 tablespoon minced tender celery leaves

Steam the potatoes for 16 to 20 minutes, until easily pierced with the blade of a knife.

Meanwhile, shell the oysters and put them with their liquid into a small nonaluminum saucepan. Place over medium heat and simmer for 30 seconds. Lift the oysters out of the saucepan with a slotted spoon and transfer to a bowl. Cover to keep them warm.

Pour off the juice from the oysters — about ⅔ cup (5 fl oz/155 ml) — and strain. Pour it back into the rinsed saucepan and boil to reduce it to 1 tablespoon of syrupy liquid. Add the vinegar and boil for 30 seconds; remove from the heat.

Wash the truffle by brushing it under running water. Peel it and keep the skin for another use. Grate it on a truffle grater, or slice it paper-thin

Warm oyster salad

using a small knife. Cut the potatoes into thin slices while they are still hot. Put them into a salad bowl and add the truffle slices.

Pour the oil into the saucepan containing the reduced oyster liquid and vinegar and whisk with a fork. Sprinkle half of this mixture over the potatoes and truffles and mix with care.

Divide the truffled potatoes among 4 plates and garnish with the warm oysters. Sprinkle the remaining vinaigrette over and scatter the celery leaves on top. Serve at once, and add pepper before eating.

LOBSTER GRATIN

Homard gratiné   Serves 4

Like crayfish, the lobster (which prefers colder waters) is a symbol of good living. It must be cooked alive so that the flesh retains its flavor. It has been a star of *grande cuisine* for nearly 300 years, and used to be an important element of sumptuous meals on fast days when no meat could be eaten — the days on which the humble poor had to be content with dried herring.

2 live lobsters, about 1½ lb (750 g) each

1 shallot, minced

½ teaspoon freshly ground black pepper

24 tarragon leaves, chopped

3 tablespoons dry white vermouth

1½ tablespoons (1 fl oz/30 ml) thick crème fraîche

¼ cup (2 oz/60 g) butter

Drop the live lobsters into boiling well-salted water in a large stockpot, cover with a lid and let return to a boil. Boil for 10 minutes. Drain the lobsters and refresh under running water.

Preheat the broiler (grill) to high heat.

In a small nonaluminum saucepan, combine the shallot, pepper, tarragon and vermouth and cook over gentle heat until all the liquid evaporates. Add the *crème fraîche* and boil for 1 minute. Whisk in the butter. Remove from the heat.

Cut the lobsters lengthwise in half and arrange them in an ovenproof dish. Detach the meat from the shells and brush the shells with half the tarragon sauce. Cut the flesh of each lobster into 6 chunks and return them to the shells.

Coat the lobsters with the remaining sauce. Put the dish under the broiler (grill) and broil (grill) for 2 minutes, to form a crust. Divide among 4 plates and serve immediately.

Lobster gratin (left); Langoustines with sea-urchins (right)

LANGOUSTINES WITH SEA-URCHINS

Langoustines aux oursins   Serves 4

The sea-urchin is a strange shellfish bristling with spikes: it looks like a large prickly ball. Its coral is very tasty and reputed to be an aphrodisiac. It is always included in any self-respecting French seafood platter, and here marries perfectly with the flavor of langoustines.

12 sea-urchins

¼ cup (2 oz/60 g) butter

12 large langoustines (Dublin Bay prawns, shrimp or scampi)

salt and freshly ground pepper

Open the sea-urchins and reserve their liquid; strain. Mix the corals with half of the butter using a mortar and pestle or a blender.

Preheat the broiler (grill) to high heat.

Cut each langoustine lengthwise in half and place, cut side up, in an ovenproof dish. Melt the rest of the butter and brush the langoustine meat with it. Season with salt and pepper.

Slide the dish under the hot broiler and cook for 4 to 5 minutes, or until the meat pulls away from the shell. Take the dish from the broiler and spread the sea-urchin butter over the langoustine meat. Broil again for 10 seconds.

Transfer the langoustines to 4 plates and serve immediately.

Note: Crayfish or lobsters may be prepared in the same manner.

SEAFOOD SALAD

Fruits de mer en salade   Serves 6

Fruits de mer is one of the really picturesque expressions of the French language. All these shellfish — crustaceans and mollusks — offer an incredible wealth and diversity of flavors. Wonderful seafood platters served in restaurants are delectable pyramids composed of every creature that lives in the sea, that is edible, and that is not a fish; absolute freshness is vital. Shellfish are an important element in making up a large menu. And, as in this recipe, they lend themselves well to subtle combinations.

1½ lb (750 g) mussels

2 tablespoons (2 fl oz/60 ml) dry white wine

10 oz (315 g) raw white squid

1 egg yolk

1 teaspoon Dijon mustard

⅓ cup (3 fl oz/90 ml) olive oil

1 small garlic clove, crushed

10 oz (315 g) cooked langoustine (Dublin Bay prawn, shrimp, or chopped scampi) meat, or langouste (spiny lobster)

10 oz (315 g) tomatoes, peeled, seeded and diced

leaves from 6 chervil sprigs

leaves from 3 tarragon sprigs

1 tablespoon chopped chives

Scrub the mussels, rinse and drain them. Put them into a 9½ inch (24 cm) nonstick sauté pan with the wine, and place on high heat. When the mussels have opened, tip them into a strainer over a large bowl. Shell them, reserving their juices. Strain the liquid into the sauté pan.

Cut the squid into very thin strips. Add to the sauté pan and cook on high heat for 5 minutes, turning with a spatula. Remove the squid with tongs and drain the strips in a colander.

Boil to reduce the cooking liquid to 3 tablespoons. Set aside to cool.

Beat the egg yolk and mustard together in a bowl with high, straight sides. Add the oil in a thin stream, beating continuously, to make a thick mayonnaise. Stir in the garlic and the squid cooking liquid; blend thoroughly.

Dress the shellfish with the sauce and mix well. Add the tomatoes, chervil, tarragon and chives. Mix well.

Serve the seafood on a green salad dressed with olive oil and lemon juice.

Preparing to go fishing, C. Roussel (1861–?); MUSEE DES BEAUX-ARTS, TOURCOING

Seafood salad

Crayfish in wine sauce

SEA CRAYFISH IN WINE SAUCE

Petites langoustes au banyuls   Serves 4

The sea crayfish (spiny lobster), like the truffle and the lobster, is a symbol of luxury and refinement in the French gastronomic imagination. This delectable crustacean, which thrives in warm seas, has become a party dish, a dish for special occasions, probably just as important for what it represents as for its taste.

2 sea crayfish (spiny lobsters) or lobsters, about 1 lb (500 g) each

½ cup (3½ oz/100 g) long-grain rice

2 tablespoons (1 oz/30 g) wild rice

2 tablespoons (1 oz/30 g) butter

1½ tablespoons peanut (groundnut) oil

1 shallot, minced

6 large and 12 small tarragon leaves

salt and freshly ground pepper

4 pinches ground cayenne pepper

½ cup (4 fl oz/125 ml) thick crème fraîche

½ cup (4 fl oz/125 ml) young Banyuls wine or other sweet white muscat

2 slices blood orange, halved

2 slices lemon, halved

Drop the crayfish into boiling salted water in a large stockpot and bring back to a boil. Simmer gently for 10 minutes. Remove the crayfish from the pot and refresh under running water for about 2 minutes. Spread them out on a board, unrolling the tails. Leave them for at least 30 minutes to cool completely.

Remove the tails and shell the crayfish, collecting the crayfish liquid as you work. Use a small spoon to take out the creamy parts and coral found in the trunk, and put them in a blender. Blend to a thin creamy consistency. Set aside in a bowl.

Discard the head and tail carapaces but keep the claws, the feelers and the cartilaginous parts of the trunk and break them up.

Preheat the oven to 400°F (200°C/Gas 6).

Cook both rices in boiling salted water until just tender and drain. Stir in the butter, mix them together and put them in the oven in a covered casserole to keep warm.

Heat the oil in a sauté pan. Drop in the claws, feelers and trunks. Brown for 5 minutes over medium heat, turning often. Add the shallot, the 6 large tarragon leaves, salt, pepper and cayenne.

Cook for 2 minutes, stirring constantly. Add the liquid from the crayfish, the *crème fraîche* and the wine and mix. As the mixture comes to a boil, crush the pieces of shell. When boiling, cover the pot and cook for 10 minutes.

Push the contents of the pot through a strainer placed over a saucepan. Let the pieces of crayfish drain thoroughly and then discard them. Add the blended coral cream and 3 half slices each of the orange and lemon. Heat gently for 3 minutes.

Divide the rice among 4 ceramic ramekins. Cut the crayfish tails into ⅛ inch (3 mm) thick rounds, and arrange on top of the rice. Coat with the sauce, and place a half-slice of orange and lemon on each. Put the ramekins in the hot oven, turn the oven off and leave the dishes to heat for 5 minutes.

Remove them from the oven, garnish each with 3 tarragon leaves and serve immediately.

CRAB MOLDS WITH CORAL SAUCE

Flans de crabe, sauce corail   Serves 6

Large *tourteau* crabs have always been appreciated in the coastal provinces. They are brown, very fleshy and sweet tasting. They have been offered at fish stalls since medieval times, and since the seventeenth century numerous recipes have been dedicated to them — primarily to meet the needs of meatless fast days. The traditional popular way of eating them in France is simple: after boiling they are shelled, and the flesh and coral are eaten with a mayonnaise sauce. However, both classical and modern cuisine offer an amazing array of recipes for this crustacean.

1 large female crab, about 2½ lb (1.2 kg), cooked (see note below)
5 eggs
salt and freshly ground pepper
¾ cup (6½ fl oz/200 ml) milk
1 tablespoon (½ fl oz/15 ml) thick crème fraîche
1 teaspoon Dijon mustard
2 pinches curry powder

Shell the crab. Shred the white meat contained in the trunk, claws and nippers into a bowl. Place the coral and creamy parts in a blender.

Preheat the oven to 350°F (180°C/Gas 4).

Break the eggs into a bowl and beat them with a fork. Add salt and pepper to taste and ⅔ cup (5 fl oz/155 ml) of the milk. Beat again, then add the

reserved white crabmeat shredded as finely as possible.

Butter six 3 inch (8 cm) ramekins and divide the mixture among them. Place them in a baking dish and add hot water to reach ½ inch (1 cm) below the rim of the molds. Bake for about 20 minutes, until the eggs have set.

Meanwhile, add the rest of the milk, the *crème fraîche*, mustard, curry powder and a little salt to the blender with the coral. Blend to a smooth purée. Pour the coral sauce into a saucepan.

When the eggs are cooked, heat the sauce gently. Remove the molds from the oven and turn out onto 6 plates. Coat with the sauce and garnish with crab claws and green tops of scallions, plunged into cold water to curl. Serve immediately

Note: In making this delicious appetizer it is important to use a female crab that is full of coral. Females are recognizable by the two orifices that will be found under the carapace when you lift the little tongue, which is, in fact, the tail.

Crab molds with coral sauce

95

The miraculous catch (detail), Jean Baptiste Jouvenet (1644–1717); THE LOUVRE, PARIS

F ISH

ith both an Atlantic and a Mediterranean coast, France has never been short of fish. Nevertheless the country is extensive, and for many inland regions it is only in the past century that supplies of fresh fish have arrived with any regularity. And yet this was an ingredient of prime importance. Indeed, during the medieval centuries the obligation to abstain from meat (and animal products) covered practically one-third of the year. As well as the days of Lent, there were two meatless days each week, plus the occasional eve of a special day such as a saint's day. Fish therefore was the only solution. Given the difficulties of transport and communication in this era, people who lived some distance from the coast appreciated the advantages of freshwater fish, which were fresh, abundant and theoretically available. However, the lords of the manors paid close attention to their rivers and ponds where the peasants were constantly poaching, and the ordinary people had the greatest difficulty obtaining this kind of food. That left only fish from the sea which had to be preserved by salting and drying.

In Paris there was a fish market near the Grand Pont. The fish was brought to Paris along the river in large baskets, covered with salt to retard spoilage, but when it arrived it was always a little bit off. The best ones, that is, those that had remained freshest, were destined for the King's household. On the fish stalls could be found porpoise, dogfish, bream, and red bream, sea bass, gurnard, mackerel, sardines, and anchovies, not to mention whale. The porpose and whale were at that time believed to be fish, because they lived in the sea — likewise the *macreuse* (scoter or surf-duck), an aquatic bird which could be eaten on meatless days. Whale blubber, *crapois*, was used as a cooking fat in poor households during Lent.

It must be emphasized, however, that fresh fish was a rarity and reserved for the privileged. The majority of people had to be satisfied with salted and dried fish. Demand for these products was enormous, in view of the number of days when meat was forbidden. This gave rise to a phenomenonal industry, especially concerning the herring. Just think, in the year 1477 at Dieppe, 177 boats brought in nearly 5,000,000 herring. The fish were then salted, and from the fifteenth century this salting was done on the boats themselves, which meant that the boats could go further out to sea. Another herring product was known as *soré*: the fish was lightly salted, then desalted before being smoked over beech or oak wood, which prevented it from spoiling. Herring has been food for the poor for many

Cook returning from market, Etienne Jeaurat (1699–1789); MUSEE DES BEAUX-ARTS, BESANCON
Jeaurat was both a history and a genre painter, and was especially fond of depicting Parisian street-life, the markets, and their people.

centuries. This product became indeed so vital that the Church allowed fishing on Sundays and holy days. This whole industry had so much influence that it could be said that herrings could decide the fate of empires. The trade in this humble fish established the power of great Northern cities such as Amsterdam. The Dutch had discovered an excellent way of preserving it, by packing it into wooden crates and steeping it in brine so it was easier to transport and kept longer. Other fish were similarly preserved in salt, particularly cod, which was dried after salting. For some reason the Southern French have always preferred dried cod to dried herring. Under the name of "stockfish" (from the nordic *stükfis* meaning fish stick, which was a literal description of this product which is as hard as wood) or *morue*, it could be just salted, or salted and then dried, or simply wind dried. Perhaps this Southern preference began when in the fifteenth century the Portuguese, followed by the Basque, went as far as Newfoundland to bring back boatloads of this essential Lenten fare.

Later, more sophisticated ways of preserving were found, as shown by this recipe of the seventeenth century given in *The Cuisinier François* by La Varenne: "take some soles, they should be very fresh. After having coated them with flour, fry them lightly in half butter and half oil. Place them in an earthen pot with salt, crushed cloves, orange and lemon rind, and cover with vinegar. Finish cooking them when serving them."

Fishing for cod, Ambroise-Louis Garneray (1783–1857); MUSEE DES BEAUX-ARTS, ROUEN France was once the only country to undertake separate fishing expeditions for fresh cod, and for cod that was salted on board. Today, freezing or salting takes place on the same boat.

But the one fish that symbolizes Lent and the ordinary foods of the medieval era is without doubt the salted herring. It is easier to understand the excesses of the populace during Mardi Gras when it is realized that this was a prelude to the Lenten menu based on a foul-smelling and often rancid fish. From these distant memories, today we have the excellent pickled herring, marinated in oil and accompanied by potatoes, and occasionally too the salted cod, cooked with onions. In the south of France there is the *brandade*, a kind of purée of salt cod and potatoes, and the *estoufinade*, a variant of the *brandade* in which olive oil is replaced by walnut oil. These two preparations do credit to the inventive spirit of our ancestors who had to deal with basic ingredients as unappealing as dried fish.

The written recipes of this time are mostly for fresh fish, since they relate to the cuisine of the wealthy classes: the fish was fried, poached, and boiled, and it was served with a concentrated sauce or as a *potage*. A characteristic sauce was the "white sauce," slightly sour because of the addition of verjuice, but smoothed out with a substantial amount of butter making it the ancestor of our *beurre blanc*. It was recommended (and so it should have been) as an accompaniment to freshwater pike.

Ducks and fish (detail), Jean-Baptiste Oudry (1686–1755);
MUSEE DES BEAUX-ARTS, DIJON
Eel was popular during the Middle Ages. Taillevent gave several recipes for it in his *Viandier* and included it in tarts, broths, a roulade, and a Lenten flan. There are numerous regional dishes such as *anguille en vert*, eel cooked in a sauce of spinach, sorrel, parsley, and sage.

Household utensils with herring, Jean
Baptiste Siméon Chardin (1699–1779);
MUSEE DE PICARDIE, AMIENS
In 1170 Louis VII granted letters patent to
a guild of dealers in saltwater fish.
Members of this guild were known as
harengères (herring-sellers), while the
name *poissoniers* (fishmongers) denoted
those who dealt solely in freshwater fish.

Up to the nineteenth century, eels were very popular. There are numerous recipes
from the Middle Ages on, mostly stews, often laced with red wine. But today it would be
difficult indeed to find eels on the average restaurant's menu. The French have been
following the general trend of contemporary societies in their fear of fat! And they have
lost their taste for this very fatty fish which, for Northern Europeans, is still considered a
delicacy.

Only slowly did consumption of fresh fish expand, naturally in line with the development of more rapid means of communication and the establishment of the *chasse marée*
(services for the transport of fish) from the English Channel. Wealthy households could sign
contracts with suppliers who agreed to supply fish still alive, in regulation containers. It
was because the fish failed to arrive, as the contract stipulated, that Vatel, maître d'hotel
to the Prince de Condé, resorted to suicide. He had been charged with organizing a feast

in the château of Chantilly at which King Louis XIV and his court were due to appear, and it so happened that the guests were more numerous than anticipated. Vatel had extraordinary organizational gifts and was coping with the situation, but he was at the point of exhaustion, his nerves on edge. He admitted he had not slept for twelve nights. At four o'clock in the morning when he was still scurrying about arranging the next day's meal, he looked everywhere to see if the *marée*, the fish order, had arrived. Here is what happened then, in the words of Madame de Sévigné who relayed the news to her daughter: "... he met a young purveyor who was bringing only two loads of fish and asked 'is that all?' The young man replied 'yes, sir,' not knowing that Vatel had placed orders at every sea port. Vatel waited a little while longer; the other purveyors were nowhere to be seen; he became agitated, believing that there would be no other deliveries; he found Gourville and said to him: 'Monsieur, I cannot survive this insult; my honor and reputation will be lost.' Vatel went upstairs to his room, placed his sword against the door and ran himself through the heart; but it was only at the third attempt, for he made two attempts which were not fatal; then he fell down dead. However, the supplies of fish arrived from all quarters; people looked for Vatel, who was to distribute it; they went to his room, knocked, forced open the door, and they found him drowned in his own blood; they hurried with the news to the Prince of Condé, who was deeply shocked ..."

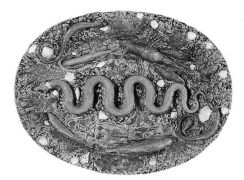

Large oval platter, attributed to Bernard Palissy (*circa* 1510–90); THE LOUVRE, PARIS
This French master potter was renowned for his vibrant polychrome glaze colors, probably influenced by his earlier work as a stained-glass artist. The frogs, fish, snakes, and foliage that crowd his pieces were cast from life. He was given the title "inventor of the king's rustic pottery."

During this period, cooks demonstrated increasing attention to the preparation of seafood. Right up to the seventeenth century the markets still sold whale and porpoise, whose darkish flesh was beginning to seem distasteful. Salmon, which was very common in all the rivers, was only moderately appreciated, to the extent that servants and laborers requested that they be served salmon not more than three times a week! Saltwater fish was always preferred by the aristocracy, since freshwater fish was thought too coarse and tasteless for delicate palates.

As fish was one of the ingredients that most stimulated culinary creativity, recipes multiplied and dishes became more sophisticated. From the seventeenth century on, the menus for meatless days represented veritable feasts. Saltwater fish were clearly the preferred varieties, and eighteenth-century gourmets appreciated turbot, began to like salmon, demanded lobsters, freshwater crayfish and crabs, and consumed vast quantities of oysters. Even the poor no longer ate the coarse flesh of whale and porpoise, although the perpetual salted herring was still a last recourse.

Later on, at the beginning of the nineteenth century, there developed in the upper classes, a taste for small, light, and delicate meals, prepared for a very few guests, all men, all gourmets and preferably good friends. Carême, who was the star cook of the period was very much in favor of making fish the main feature of this kind of meal, and he gladly presented turbot, salmon, and lobsters from Cherbourg, shrimp from Honfleur and smelt from the mouth of the Seine. "Salmon and turbot," he wrote, "should be cooked quickly and well covered by the liquid, in these matured wines which set in train the digestive actions of the stomach."

In the same century a new method of preserving fish by canning was to end the supremacy of dried herring and cod. In Brittany, along the rocky coasts, sprang up the first sardine canneries, and they made the fortune of the area for many years. Sardines in oil became extremely popular, appeared on all the tables, and even became a classic ingredient of *hors d'oeuvres*.

Consumption of fresh fish continued to increase slowly in succeeding centuries. From 5 lb (2.4 kg) per person per year in 1781–89, it rose to 26 lb (12 kg) in the 1960s. It was during the 1970s, however, that fish consumption took a real leap as the French, who still generally considered fish a "penitential" food, began to eat it more and more frequently, for reasons of both health and taste. Credit should also be given to the culinary revolution that began with Nouvelle Cuisine.

Fish has always had a role in the traditional order of a meal, be it for a "meat" or "meatless" day. It used to precede the poultry dish and the roast of meat. Certain dishes, such as *bouillabaisse* from the Marseille region, have become classics. This fish soup is a complete meal in itself: fish from the rocky shores and the deep sea are cooked in a saffron-flavored stock and served with the celebrated *rouille*, a garlic sauce made with egg yolks and olive oil and heightened with chili. The *bourride* is another great fish soup, with garlic and olive oil, which is a specialty of the Languedoc coast. Actually all sea towns in France have their own version of fish soup, varying from the garlic and tomato flavor of

Eel and red mullet, Edouard Manet (1832–83); MUSEE D'ORSAY, PARIS
The Ancient Greeks held the red mullet in such esteem that they dedicated it to Hecate, while the Romans were prepared to pay outrageous prices for it. The colour varies from bright pink to reddish brown, the former being considered superior.

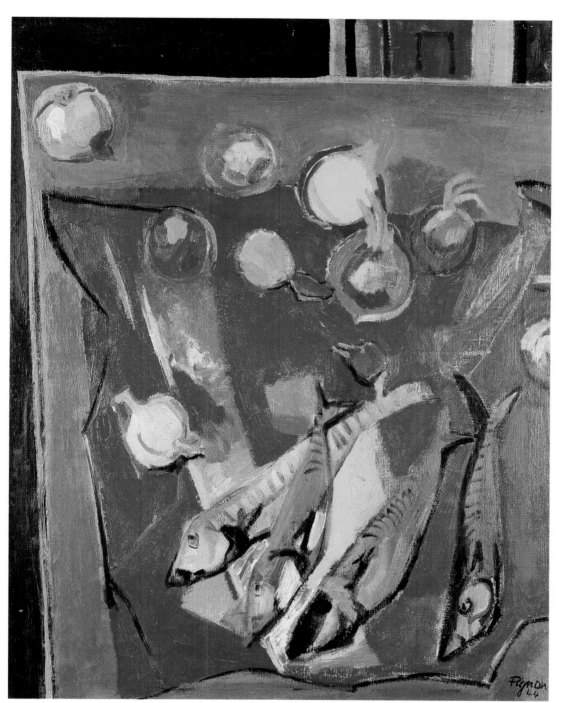

Mackerel contain a high percentage of fat which causes them to spoil quickly. The freshest mackerel were once sold in France as hunting-horn mackerel, denoting that less than twenty-four hours had elapsed since their capture. The arrival of fresh fish from the coast used to be announced by the blast of a horn — hence the name.

the South, to cream and white wine added in the North. Anchovies, previously known to the inland population only in their salted form, are a specialty of the Catalan coast; together with capers and tomatoes, they were typical ingredients of Mediterranean France, and they became part of classical cuisine after the Revolution.

Towards the North, around Brittany and Normandy, there is the pike, king of river fish, which is accompanied by a *beurre blanc* sauce, flavored with excellent vinegar and shallots. A recipe for a very similar sauce appears in a collection dated to about 1400. Amongst other traditional dishes are *matelote d'anguilles*, eel stew in a red wine sauce, and *pochouse*, another dish using freshwater fish — both dishes originating in the center of France and in Burgundy. Nor should one forget *sole normande*, cooked in the style of Normandy with the obligatory cream; or *truites au bleu*, fresh trout which have barely left their mountain streams to be quickly poached in an aromatic *court bouillon*.

Herbed baby mackerel

HERBED BABY MACKEREL

Lisettes aux aromates   Serves 4

Lisettes are tiny mackerel with a very delicate flesh. One very old method of cooking mackerel to preserve it was to cook it in white wine and vinegar. Prepared this way it would keep for several days. It is a method similar to that of preparing *escabeche* (fried fish soused with vinegar and spices), of the Midi, a dish that is also found in Belgium, probably due to the influence of Spanish invaders in the past. Today mackerel in white wine is a regional specialty of the Normandy coast. This recipe is inspired by the classic method, to which it adds further flavor and refinement.

8 small mackerel, about 3½ oz (100 g) each,
    cleaned, with heads removed
¼ cup (2 oz/60 g) coarse sea salt
2 thyme sprigs
3 bay leaves
4 whole cloves
1 teaspoon freshly ground pepper
1 teaspoon coriander seeds
1¼ cups (10 fl oz/315 ml) cider vinegar
½ lemon, thinly sliced
12 fresh shallots, peeled

Wash the mackerel and pat dry. Place on a plate, scatter with the coarse salt and set aside to macerate for 4 hours.

Preheat the oven to 350°F (180°C/Gas 4).

Rinse the mackerel and pat dry. Lay them head-to-tail in a long terrine, layering the thyme, bay leaves, cloves, pepper and coriander in

between. Add the vinegar and ⅓ cup (3 fl oz/90 ml) water or a little more, sufficient to cover the fish. Add the lemon and shallots to the terrine.

Cover the terrine with a sheet of foil and place in a hot *bain-marie:* put the terrine in a large ovenproof pan and fill the large pan with just-boiled water to reach halfway up the sides of the terrine. Put it in the oven for 30 minutes; the *bain-marie* liquid should barely simmer.

When the fish are cooked, take the terrine from the oven and let the fish cool in their juices to room temperature, then refrigerate for 1 hour. Serve cold, basted with the juices and surrounded with lemon and shallots.

MACKEREL WITH GOOSEBERRIES

Maqueraux aux groseilles   Serves 4

In the middle of the seventeenth century François-Pierre La Varenne wrote a cookbook called *Le Cuisinier François*, which became a bestseller. This recipe is taken from the book, and is a classic among classics. The debate will continue as to whether *groseilles à maqueraux* (the full French name for gooseberries) are so named because traditionally they accompanied mackerel, or whether, as some maintain, *maqueraux* once meant "stripes" and referred to the streaking on the skin of these large juicy berries and to the dark lines on the sides of the fish. In this recipe, the sharp sauce evokes something of medieval culinary tastes.

> They must be roasted with fennel; once cooked, open them and take out the backbone, and make a good sauce with butter, parsley and gooseberries; when it is all seasoned, bring it to a boil, let it bubble for a moment, then serve your mackerel with your sauce.

4 mackerel, about 6½ oz (200 g) each, filleted
salt and freshly ground pepper
2 tablespoons peanut (groundnut) oil
¼ cup (2 oz/60 g) butter
2 tablespoons aged wine vinegar
1 teaspoon superfine (caster) sugar
8 oz (250 g) gooseberries, topped and tailed
leaves from 2 tarragon sprigs

Wash and dry the fish fillets. Make 4 incisions in the skin side of each. Season on both sides with salt and pepper.

into a nonreactive 9½ inch (24 cm) casserole and place over gentle heat. Let them dry out for a few minutes, stirring constantly, then pour in 2 cups (16 fl oz/500 ml) of the wine. As soon as it boils, add the carrot, tomato, thyme, bay leaf, parsley, pepper and garlic. Let it boil and reduce for 20 minutes, until dry. Add the remaining wine and 1 cup (8 fl oz/250 ml) of water. Bring to a boil; add the veal stock and boil to reduce by half, about 15 minutes.

Add the cinnamon, mace, nutmeg, sugar and lime zest. Simmer for 3 minutes, then strain the sauce into a nonreactive small saucepan and keep hot.

Cook the salmon. Wipe the steaks dry. Put them in a 10¼ inch (26 cm) nonstick skillet, skin down, and cook over medium heat for 5 minutes. Cover and cook for another 2 minutes. Divide the salmon among 4 hot plates.

Whisk the butter into the hot sauce and surround the salmon steaks with it.

Serve immediately with grated potato cakes or potatoes.

MARINATED SALMON

Saumon mariné   Serves 4

Raw or marinated fish was a novelty introduced to the French table following the Nouvelle Cuisine revolution. The inspiration for these preparations is Scandinavian or Japanese, and they have been so well accepted by the French as to have become part of our contemporary culinary tradition.

1 piece of fresh salmon cut from the fillet, about 13 oz (410 g), boned, with skin left on
2 tablespoons coarse sea salt
1 tablespoon superfine (caster) sugar
4 dill sprigs
3 tablespoons extra virgin olive oil
1 teaspoon finely and freshly ground pepper
1 tablespoon snipped chives
1 tablespoon snipped dill

Wash the salmon, which after boning will be in two pieces, and pat dry. Sprinkle the salt and sugar over the fish and lay the dill sprigs on top, crushing them between your fingers. Place the two pieces of fish back together, skin side out, to return the slice to its original shape. Wrap the fish in 2 sheets of plastic film and refrigerate for 12 hours.

Rinse the fish thoroughly. Place one piece on a board, skin side down. Cut it into thin slices using a very sharp knife, holding the blade almost parallel to the board; do not break the skin, it will remain on the board when you have finished cutting. Divide the slices among 4 plates.

In a bowl, combine the oil, pepper, chives and dill. Coat the salmon slices with this sauce. Refrigerate for 1 hour before serving.

Accompany with toast or slices of rye bread or cumin bread, small green tomatoes and little sticks of cucumber or celery.

The fisherman, illustration from the fifteenth-century manuscript *The Great Herbal;* ESTE LIBRARY, MODENA

John Dory with tomato vinaigrette

JOHN DORY WITH TOMATO VINAIGRETTE

Saint Pierre à la vinaigrette de tomates   Serves 3

To see this fish with its hang-dog look, it is hard to believe that its flesh is exquisite. Yet in the last few years it has become a sort of culinary star, along with turbot and sea perch (which in the Mediterranean is also known as *loup de mer*, literally "sea wolf.")

For a long time the traditional way of serving John Dory has been with a purée of sorrel, and while it is very good served that way, it is even better with a light aromatic sauce such as the one in this recipe — a perfect example of the current development in sauces in France.

1 John Dory, about 2 lb (1 kg), filleted and skinned
salt and freshly ground pepper
2 tablespoons extra virgin olive oil
1 tablespoon balsamic or aged wine vinegar
8 oz (250 g) perfectly ripe tomatoes, peeled,
    seeded and finely diced
12 kalamata (black) olives, pitted and thinly sliced
4 scallions (spring onions), halved lengthwise and
    thinly sliced (the white and the green)
12 basil leaves, minced

Lightly season the fish fillets with salt and pepper.

Heat the oil in a 10¼ inch (26 cm) nonstick skillet. Add the fillets and cook for 3 minutes on each side over medium heat; remove them from the pan and discard the cooking oil. Keep the fish warm.

Pour the vinegar into the pan and cook until evaporated. Add the tomatoes and olives and cook for 2 minutes stirring. Season with salt and pepper. Add the scallions and stir for 30 seconds. Add the basil and stir for 30 seconds more.

Coat the fillets with the tomato vinaigrette and serve warm or cold.

SEA BREAM BAKED WITH LEMON

Daurade au citron   Serves 2

The French, on the whole, have always preferred ocean fish to freshwater varieties. One author wrote in the sixteenth century that river fish "is too coarse, it encumbers the limbs and swells them with a heavy tumescence . . ." And still today at fish markets it is ocean fish that win the limelight. Sea bream is one of the most commonly used varieties for baking in the oven.

1 sea bream (porgy), about 2 lb (1 kg), cleaned
    and scaled
2 tablespoons coarse sea salt
1 large lemon, thinly sliced
1 tablespoon freshly ground black pepper
2 tablespoons extra virgin olive oil

Wash and dry the fish. Sprinkle both sides with 1 tablespoon of salt. Sprinkle the rest of the salt over the lemon slices. Set the fish and lemon slices aside to macerate for 1 hour; then rinse and pat dry.

Preheat the oven to 475°F (240°C/Gas 9). Make 3 incisions on each side of the fish and insert a lemon slice in each. Season both sides of the fish with pepper.

Lightly oil a large sheet of parchment (baking) paper and lay half the remaining lemon slices on it. Place the bream on top and cover it with the rest of the lemon slices. Coat with the remaining oil. Close the paper around the fish and fold to seal well. Bake for 15 minutes.

When the bream is cooked, open the paper case and divide the lemon slices between 2 plates. Lift the fillets from the fish and place them on top of the lemon slices. Coat with the accumulated cooking juices. Serve at once, adding pepper before eating.

Swiss Chard (silverbeet) with Anchovies (p.187), Eggplant (aubergine) Purée (p.195), or braised fennel are suitable accompaniments.

Sea bream baked with lemon (left); Sea bream baked in salt, with red pistou (right)

SEA BREAM BAKED IN SALT, WITH RED PISTOU

Daurade au gros sel, au pistou rouge　　　Serves 4

Here is another new variation on the theme of the southern *pistou*, a perfect accompaniment to sea bream. It is reminiscent of the popular *daurade à la provençale* (in which the fish is baked with tomatoes and herbs) but is a rather more refined dish.

3 lb (1.5 kg) coarse sea salt

1 sea bream (porgy), about 3 lb (1.5 kg), cleaned, with scales left on

3 tablespoons extra virgin olive oil

1 tablespoon lemon juice

salt and freshly ground pepper

11 oz (345 g) ripe tomatoes, peeled, seeded and finely chopped

24 basil leaves, chopped

Wash the fish and pat dry.

Preheat the oven to 475°F (240°C/Gas 9). Spread one-third of the sea salt over the bottom of an ovenproof dish just large enough to hold the fish. Lay the bream on the salt and cover it completely with the remaining salt. Bake in the hot oven for 40 minutes.

Meanwhile, prepare the red *pistou*. Beat together the oil, lemon juice and salt and pepper to taste. Add the tomatoes and basil. Pour into a sauceboat.

When the fish is cooked, break the crust that will have been formed by the salt, and discard it. The skin of the bream will come away with the salt, exposing the perfectly cooked fillets. Lift off the fillets onto 4 plates. Serve immediately and pass the red *pistou* sauce separately. Each diner coats the fish with the sauce before eating.

Serve with baby zucchini (courgettes) or steamed young leeks.

111

Still life with fish, Francois Mather (seventeenth century); MUSEE DES BEAUX-ARTS, NANTES

TROUT WITH LEEK CREAM SAUCE

Truites à la crème dé poireaux   Serves 2

River trout are becoming rare. To cook one of these you need first to be a good fisherman. Not only the pollution of the rivers, but poaching as well have depleted many populations of river trout. Still, the cultivated variety, which has become one of the cheapest and most plentiful fish on the market, is well suited to many methods of cooking. In this recipe the leek cream sauce transforms a modest fish into a sumptuous dish.

2 tablespoons (1 oz/30 g) butter

2 river (wild) trout, about 9 oz (280 g) each, cleaned

16 (1 lb/500 g) young leeks, cut into julienne and 12 green leaves reserved

2 pinches sugar

2 pinches grated nutmeg

1 tablespoon dry white vermouth

salt and freshly ground pepper

⅔ cup (5 fl oz/155 ml) thick crème fraîche

4 fresh dill flowers

Preheat the oven to 475°F (240°C/Gas 9). Grease two 9½ inch (24 cm) oval gratin dishes very lightly with some of the butter.

Wash the trout. Spread the leek leaves over the perforated surface of a steamer. Lay the trout head-to-tail on the leeks, put a lid on the pan and steam the fish for 10 minutes. When the trout are cooked, set aside to cool for 3 minutes. Remove their skins; lift off the fillets and lay them in the gratin dishes.

Melt the remaining butter in a 9½ inch (24 cm) nonstick skillet. Add the julienned leeks and cook, turning often, for 8 minutes with a lid half-covering the pan.

Add the sugar, nutmeg, vermouth and salt and pepper to taste. Cook, uncovered, for 2 minutes, until the vermouth evaporates. Add the *crème fraîche* and bring to a boil. Turn off the heat, add the dill and mix.

Coat the trout fillets with the contents of the pan. Put the dishes into the hot oven and bake for 10 minutes. Transfer to a serving plate and serve immediately.

TROUT WITH GREEN STUFFING

Truites farcies au vert   Serves 3

Trout is the freshwater fish most commonly eaten in France, both because of its taste and because of the existence of numerous trout farms. In every region with waterways, peasants recount stories of poaching trout by catching them by hand under the rocks in some stream.

Stuffed fish have always been an interesting delicacy in our culinary repertoire, and here the subtle green filling combines perfectly with the taste and texture of the trout.

1 tablespoon extra virgin olive oil

¼ cup (2 oz/60 g) butter

1 small onion, finely minced

8 oz (250 g) very small zucchini (courgettes), very finely grated

1 garlic clove, crushed

2 tablespoons dry breadcrumbs

salt and freshly ground pepper

2 pinches grated nutmeg

2 tablespoons snipped basil

3 trout, 9 oz (280 g) each, cleaned but left whole

2 tablespoons dry white vermouth

tarragon for garnish

Heat the oil in a 10¼ inch (26 cm) nonstick skillet and add 1 tablespoon of the butter. When melted, add the onion and cook for 3 minutes, without coloring. Add the zucchini and cook for about 10 minutes, until they stop giving off liquid.

Add the garlic and cook for 30 seconds. Stir in the breadcrumbs, salt, pepper and nutmeg. Remove the pan from the heat and turn the mixture out into a ceramic or earthenware bowl. Let it cool, and then mix in the basil.

Preheat the oven to 475°F (240°C/Gas 9). Lightly butter a 12½ inch (32 cm) baking dish. Place the trout flat on a board, skin side down, and put one-third of the stuffing in each fish. Reform the fish into their original shape. Lay them in the dish and sprinkle slivers of the remaining butter on top. Moisten with the vermouth and season with salt and pepper.

Bake for 25 minutes in the hot oven, basting twice during cooking.

Transfer the trout to 3 plates. Pour the cooking juices over them and garnish with tarragon. Serve immediately.

Trout with leek cream sauce (left); Trout with green stuffing (right)

113

BAKED TURBOT WITH BAY LEAVES

Turbot rôti au laurier   Serves 4

The turbot is such a fine fish that it hardly needs sophisticated accompaniments. Traditionally it was poached in a *court bouillon* flavored with herbs, in a specially designed pan called a *turbotière*, which echoed the flat lozenge shape of the fish itself. This recipe allows the full flavor of the turbot to be developed.

1 lemon
salt
12 fresh bay leaves, cut into thin strips
6 tablespoons extra virgin olive oil
4 turbot, halibut, plaice, flounder or sole steaks,
  about 8 oz (250 g) each, skin removed

Halve the lemon lengthwise. Put the lemon halves onto a board, cut side down, and cut each lengthwise into 4 pieces. Cut each piece into very thin fan-shaped bits. Put them into a bowl, scatter salt over, and add the bay leaf strips. Cover with ¼ cup (2 fl oz/60 ml) of the oil and set aside to marinate for 30 minutes.

Brush the fish steaks with the remaining oil and sprinkle with salt.

Preheat the oven to 475°F (240°C/Gas 9).

Pour the contents of the bowl into an ovenproof dish just large enough to hold the fish, and spread over the bottom of the dish. Lay the turbot on top with what would have been the skin side down. Bake the fish for 20 minutes.

Serve the fish hot, covered in the lemon pieces and their milky marinade. Add pepper before eating.

Serve with a potato purée with olive oil added and garnished with sliced black olives.

Baked turbot with bay leaves (left); Turbot with capers (right)

TURBOT WITH CAPERS

Turbot aux câpres   Serves 2

Towards the end of the Middle Ages turbot was frequently to be found on Paris fish stalls, and since then the fondness of the French for this fish has been well known. The following recipe is taken from *La Cuisinière Bourgeoise*, which was written by Menon in 1746 and regularly reissued for seventy years. His recipes often include typical Southern ingredients like anchovies and capers.

> Put a good lump of butter into a pot with a pinch of flour, salt, coarse pepper, an anchovy washed and chopped, and some good capers; stir the sauce until it is thick, without letting it boil, and serve it over the fish.
>
> You may also serve it with a *béchamel* sauce; reduce three-and-a-half pints of cream by half, add a little salt, and serve over the turbot.
>
> Again you can serve it with a sauce of chopped herbs, suitable for a day when you do not have meat, or with a ragoût of freshwater crayfish.

1 teaspoon Dijon mustard
1 teaspoon anchovy paste
¼ cup (2 oz/60 g) butter
grated zest (rind) and juice of 1 lemon
2 tablespoons drained capers
2 skinless fillets of turbot, halibut, plaice, flounder or sole, about 6½ oz (200 g) each
salt
1 teaspoon extra virgin olive oil

To make the sauce, combine the mustard, anchovy paste, butter and lemon zest in a nonreactive small saucepan. Add 2 tablespoons of the lemon juice and put the saucepan over very low heat. Cook, stirring constantly, until you have a thick cream: the butter should not melt enough to separate. Take the pan off the heat and add the capers.

Rinse the turbot fillets, pat them dry and salt them lightly. Pour the oil into a 9½ inch (24 cm) nonstick skillet and place over medium heat. When the oil is hot, lay the turbot fillets in the pan with what would have been the skin side down. Cover the pan with a perforated lid and cook over low heat for 8 minutes.

Transfer the fillets to 2 plates and coat them with caper sauce — it will melt slowly on contact with the hot fish — and serve at once.

Accompany with steamed green vegetables such as cauliflower, broccoli or zucchini (courgettes).

Haddock parmentier

HADDOCK PARMENTIER

Parmentier de haddock   Serves 6

Thanks to the English, haddock is now widely consumed in France, especially in the northern part of the country. Its smoky flavor is reminiscent of dried herring, but it is much sweeter. This recipe is particularly interesting because it rings changes on an ancient theme by taking its inspiration from a dish known as *brandade de morue*. The *brandade* is a creation of the Midi, a purée of potatoes enriched by a purée of salt cod that has been well cooked and flavored with garlic and olive oil. Here the haddock replaces the cod, to produce a dish with a much sweeter taste.

2 lb (1 kg) new potatoes
salt
2½ lb (1.2 kg) haddock fillets
2 garlic cloves, crushed
2 tablespoons extra virgin olive oil
sage for garnish

Wash the potatoes, place them in a large saucepan, cover with cold water and bring to a boil. Salt lightly. Cook for about 20 minutes, until soft.

Meanwhile, put the haddock fillets into a large saucepan and cover with cold water. Bring almost to a boil — as soon as the first bubbles appear, remove from the heat. Set aside for 10 minutes.

When the potatoes are cooked, drain and set aside to cool. Peel the potatoes and put them into the bowl of a food processor. Add the garlic and oil and process until smooth.

Skin and bone the haddock and add the flesh to the potato mixture. Process at high speed for 10 to 20 seconds, so the fish will disintegrate but not be reduced to a purée.

Garnish with sage and serve immediately with slices of bread spread with a purée of black olives.

115

OVEN-BAKED FRESH COD

Cabillaud boulangère   Serves 6

Fresh cod from the Northern Atlantic is the most popular everyday fish in France. It is a mainstay of the fish-vendor's business, and French fishing fleets travel to the far North to seek it out — to Labrador and Newfoundland.

In medieval times salt cod was almost as important as dried or salted herrings were, for daily fare on meatless days. And as recently as the 1950s in country areas salt cod was still synonymous with Fridays, fast days and Lent. Even barely twenty years ago in Lozère, at threshing time or harvest time it was necessary to ask the local priest for a dispensation from fasting on Fridays so that harvesters could be fed good red meat to build them up, for they felt that fish did not give them sufficient strength.

1 piece of fresh cod, about 2¾ lb (1.3 kg), cut 4 inches (10 cm) thick and 8 inches (20 cm) long (taken from the middle part of a 7 lb/3.5 kg fish)

4 dried fennel sprigs

6½ oz (200 g) very thinly sliced smoked bacon

¼ cup (2 oz/60 g) butter

2 lb (1 kg) potatoes, peeled and sliced ⅛ inch (3 mm) thick

2 fennel bulbs, coarsely shredded (grated)

salt and freshly ground pepper

Rinse the fish and pat dry. Insert the dried fennel into the stomach area; wrap the bacon slices around it and tie it up as you would a roast.

Preheat the oven to 475°F (240°C/Gas 9). Melt the butter in a large oval or rectangular baking dish. Add the potatoes to the baking dish and mix

Oven-baked fresh cod (left); Salt cod in Muscadet (right)

them with the butter. Remove the outer layers of the fennel bulbs and wash the hearts before shredding (grating) them in a cylindrical grater using a disk with large holes. Add the seasoning and shredded fennel to the potatoes and mix well. Even out the surface with a spatula.

Place the cod in the dish with the belly side up. Bake for 30 minutes. Turn the fish and bake for 30 minutes more.

When the fish is cooked, remove the string and set it on the bed of potatoes. Serve hot in the dish in which it was cooked.

Note: If you are using a smaller piece of fish, pre-cook the potatoes on their own in the oven for 10 to 15 minutes.

SALT COD IN MUSCADET

Morue en cocotte au muscadet   Serves 4

The preparation of salt cod is a delicate operation. If it is badly de-salted or cooked it can have a rancid taste that is quite abominable — in the olden days Friday with salt cod and potatoes was traditionally seen as a day of penitence! It requires time and inclination to prepare a *brandade* or a recipe like the one below, which transforms a strong-smelling, rubbery piece of salt fish into a delectable dish.

1½ lb (750 g) salt cod fillets
¼ cup (2 fl oz/60 ml) olive oil
1 small onion, sliced
1 medium leek, white part thinly sliced diagonally
1 garlic clove, minced
1 thyme sprig
1 bay leaf
1 strip of lemon zest (rind)
2 pinches saffron threads
6½ oz (200 g) tomatoes, peeled, seeded and diced
13 oz (410 g) firm-fleshed potatoes, peeled and
*   sliced paper-thin*
⅓ cup (3 fl oz/90 ml) Muscadet
salt and freshly ground pepper

Soak the cod under a thin stream of running water for 12 hours to remove the salt.

Cut each cod fillet into 4 pieces. Bring some water to a simmer in a large saucepan and drop the fish into it. Simmer for 5 minutes. Remove from the heat and drain the fish.

Heat the oil in a 6 qt (6 l) fireproof casserole and add the onion and leek. Brown for 5 minutes over gentle heat. Stir in the garlic, thyme, bay leaf,

Early morning at the fish market, Victor Gabriel Gilbert (1847–1933); MUSEE DES BEAUX-ARTS, LILLE

lemon zest and saffron. Add the tomatoes, potatoes and wine. Season with salt and pepper and pour in 1 cup (8 fl oz/250 ml) water. Bring to a boil and cook for 15 minutes.

Add the cod and cook for 10 minutes over low heat, turning the fish twice.

Lift the cod out of the casserole and arrange on 4 hot plates, surrounded with the tomato-flavored potatoes. Coat with the pan juices and serve at once with slices of toast.

The poultry seller, Albrecht Kauw, the Elder (1621–81); MUSEE DE L'OEUVRE NOTRE DAME, STRASBOURG

The midday meal, engraving by Scotin
(seventeenth century);
BIBLIOTHEQUE DES ARTS DECORATIFS, PARIS

domestic poultry. Until the discovery of the Americas, the name *coq d'Inde* (or *poule de Guinée*) meant the guineafowl, originally from Abyssinia and already familiar for several centuries. Later the name was shortened to *dinde* and applied to the turkey from America. The raising of turkeys spread rapidly throughout the whole of Europe. Fattened poultry were particularly sought after by gourmets, and to produce such succulent birds the keepers resorted to force-feeding, using a funnel to force the birds to ingest large quantities of cracked grain. The practice of force-feeding to fatten ducks, geese, and chickens is extremely ancient; it is illustrated in Egyptian art from the reign of the pharaohs. It was certainly used in France from the Gallo-Roman period. Le Ménagier de Paris, writing in about 1390, talks of people raising geese in Paris and feeding them with cereal flour to fatten them. Of course, force-feeding, whether using a funnel or not, was not only practiced to enlarge the liver of geese or ducks, but also simply to fatten the birds. The famous *poulardes* of the Bresse region, or of le Mans, were hand fed to produce large and fatty animals with tender meat. The practice was actually no more cruel than our own techniques of battery-raised poultry. It was only in the eighteenth century, however, that *foie gras* became a luxury product. Until then it had been a regional specialty of Alsace or of the Southwest and had not yet been incorporated into the *grande cuisine*. The idea of commercializing goose liver pâté in Paris is credited to an Alsatian chef belonging to the household of the Marshal de Contades; thus began its international career.

For almost a century, *foie gras* was present on the tables only in the shape of this celebrated pâté. As provincial cooking started awakening an increased interest among young chefs and gourmets, *foie gras* began to be appreciated "pure." That is, simply preserved whole in its own fat, as it is traditionally prepared in Southwest France. But the very best way of enjoying this delicacy is to have it fresh, whole, barely poached, and served as it is.

Until recently *foie gras* was just a side-dish, or part of another dish, such as in the famous *tournedos Rossini*, crowned by a slice of this luxury ingredient. It fitted the more robust appetites of our forebears, who could eat far more than we do. The chefs of Nouvelle Cuisine have given *foie gras* a new role: that of a main course. It makes a perfect central dish of a meal, its natural richness needing nothing else with it other than a light salad!

The life of Alexander the Great; How Alexander came to be poisoned;
J. Vauquelin (1460), illuminated manuscript;
MUSEE DE LA VILLE DE PARIS, PETIT PALAIS, PARIS
Alexander, a leader and conqueror of extraordinary tenacity and skill, died in Babylon of a fever in 323 BC when he was only thirty-two. The exact cause of death is not known but may have been related to something he had eaten.

salt and freshly ground pepper

1 guinea hen, about 3 lb (1.5 kg), cut into 6 pieces

2 tablespoons (1 oz/30 g) butter

2 oz (60 g) smoked bacon, minced

3 tablespoons dark muscat or port

*1¼ lb (600 g) Belgian endives (chicory, witloof),
   each cut crosswise into 8 pieces*

⅔ cup (5 fl oz/155 ml) crème fraîche

4 pinches grated nutmeg

1½ teaspoons lemon juice

Salt and pepper the guineafowl pieces. Melt the butter in an 11 inch (28 cm) nonstick sauté pan. Add the guineafowl and brown over low heat for 5 minutes. Add the bacon and cook for 10 minutes with a lid half-covering the pan, stirring frequently.

Discard the fat that accumulates in the pan. Pour in the muscat and stir as it evaporates. Add the endives and brown for 15 minutes with the pan half-covered, turning them often.

Stir in the *crème fraîche*. Sprinkle with the nutmeg and salt and pepper and cook for 15 minutes over low heat with the pan half-covered, until the cream coats the pieces of guineafowl. Add the lemon juice and stir for 30 seconds.

Transfer the guineafowl and endives to a deep plate and serve immediately.

Accompany with Potato Cakes (p.196).

Pigeon and peas (top); Guineafowl with Belgian endives (bottom)

143

Rustic meal, miniature from the *Codex Sophilogium* (late fifteenth, early sixteenth century); ARCHIVES OF TORRE DE TOMBO, LISBON

CIVET OF HARE

Civet de lièvre   Serves 6

This recipe is taken from *Le Ménagier de Paris,* which was written around 1390 by a middle-class Parisian for his very young wife. It is a cookbook and at the same time a treatise on domestic economy, the first of its kind in the French language.

Civet of hare or rabbit has been a classic dish for hundreds of years, and although the method of preparation has varied over time the basic principle of cooking in wine remains unchanged. In the original recipe the "burnt" bread, probably toasted to a very dark brown, served to give color, consistency and a bitter flavor to the sauce. Since the end of the seventeenth century this effect has been achieved by thickening the sauce with the blood of the hare. These days the liver mixed carefully into the sauce can serve as a perfect thickening agent, while the slight bitterness once contributed by the toasted bread can be imparted by two squares of bitter dark chocolate.

First of all, split the hare through the chest. If it has been killed a day or two previously, do not wash it at all but stiffen it on a broiler [grill] or over embers. Have some cooked onions and some lard in a pot and put in the hare cut into pieces. Brown it over the heat, shaking the pot very often. You can also brown it in a skillet. Then toast some bread and let it soak in meat broth with vinegar and wine.

Have ready some previously pounded ginger, Malaguetta pepper, cloves, long pepper, nutmeg and cinnamon, and steep them in verjuice and vinegar or meat broth. Set them aside. Then pound your softened bread, put it through a sieve with the stock, add the onions, the lard and the hare, the spices, and some pounded burnt bread. Cook all this together and make sure the stew is dark, acidulated with vinegar, seasoned with salt and spices. Rabbit stew is also made as above.

---

1 small shallot, chopped
salt and freshly ground pepper
4 pinches ground allspice
1 thyme sprig
2 bay leaves

7 tablespoons extra virgin olive oil
2 tablespoons aged wine vinegar
1 hare, about 4 lb (2 kg), cut into 8 pieces, with liver reserved
2 tablespoons (1 oz/30 g) butter
8 oz (250 g) bacon, cut into julienne
1 medium onion, coarsely chopped
1 medium carrot, coarsely chopped
1 tablespoon all-purpose (plain) flour
1 garlic clove, crushed
2 cups (16 fl oz/500 ml) chicken consommé
3 cups (24 fl oz/750 ml) dry red wine
2 teaspoons old Armagnac

Prepare the marinade a day in advance. In a large bowl, combine the shallot, salt and pepper, allspice, thyme and bay leaves crumbled in your fingers, ¼ cup (2 fl oz/60 ml) of the oil, and the vinegar. Blend together with a fork. Add the pieces of hare, stir, and cover. Refrigerate for 6 to 8 hours, turning the hare in the marinade from time to time.

The next day, drain the pieces of hare and wipe them with paper towels. Preheat the oven to 300°F (150°C/Gas 2).

Pour the remaining 3 tablespoons of oil into a 6 qt (6 l) cast-iron casserole and add the butter. As soon as it melts, add the bacon and the chopped onion and carrot. Brown for 5 minutes, stirring all the while; remove with a slotted spoon. Place the hare in the casserole and brown on all sides. Return the onion and carrot mixture to the casserole, season with salt and pepper and sprinkle with the flour. Cook, stirring, for 2 minutes. Add the garlic, consommé and wine. Bring to a boil, stirring. Cover the casserole and put it into the hot oven. Cook for 2 hours.

At the end of 2 hours take the casserole from the oven and drain the pieces of hare; keep warm. Strain the cooking juices into a saucepan and reduce over medium heat until about 1½ cups (13 fl oz/410 ml) remain.

Clean the liver, cut it into 4 pieces and put it into the bowl of a food processor. Add half of the reduced cooking juices and the Armagnac. Mix till smooth. With the processor running, gradually add the remaining juices until you have a thick sauce.

Coat the hare pieces with the sauce and serve immediately.

Serve with glazed mushrooms and onions, Mashed Potatoes (p. 196) or braised chestnuts.

Civet of hare

A halt during hunting, Carle van Loo (1705–65); THE LOUVRE, PARIS Made principal painter to the king in 1762, van Loo was considered the leading history painter of his day.

o painted portraits and decorative works.

The meat-day lunch, Alexandre-François Desportes (1661–1743); PRIVATE COLLECTION The hams produced by the Gauls probably tasted very similar to those consumed today. They were salted for two or three days prior to smoking, then rubbed with oil and vinegar and hung up to dry. Ham was eaten at the beginning of a meal to stimulate the tastebuds, or at the end to bring on a thirst.

country rustics). But it was not "natural," particularly for meats. Cooks, far from wanting to retain the original appearance and flavor of their ingredients, went to great lengths to disguise and mask their dishes. They prepared "beef to look like bear meat" and "mock veal" from sturgeon. The taste for simpler dishes did not develop until the seventeenth century.

Meat consumption varied according to social status and season. Pork was eaten by peasants who raised pigs, killing and salting them at the start of winter. One of the products was *bacon,* an old French word meaning salted pork, which was taken over by the English and later readopted by the French in the guise of an Anglo-Saxon borrowing. In ancient Gaul there had been a *"Dieu Bacon,"* a god in the form of a pig or wild boar. The Gauls were famous for their salted hams and left a legacy of their skills; the hams from Bayonne, among others, have continued to uphold the French reputation for charcuterie. Anthimus, writing in the sixth century, noted that the French predilection for salted pork "went beyond all description." All through the Middle Ages the taste for ham was predominant in the rural diet. It was a complementary staple, a food which kept for winter use, or in periods of need, as important for the small farmers as for the rich landowners. We find hams pictured in early manuscripts, on the stained-glass windows of cathedrals, on bas-reliefs, in a word, on every surface medieval people chose to picture themselves in their seasonal activities. In Paris, every year, there was a ham fair, held in front of Notre Dame cathedral (this tradition has survived to the present day in other fairs around Paris, such as in the little town of Chatou). This very French taste was expressed vividly a few centuries later (in the sixteenth century) by King Henri IV, who, admiring the beautiful painted ceilings of the Louvre palace, exclaimed: "A few hams hanging over there would be even more to my taste!" As centuries go by, the taste remains, and the famous Grimod de La Reynière, our first food writer of the end of the eighteenth century, inscribes ham as one of the cardinal virtues of spring (together with leg of lamb). He also gives a marvelous description of what he calls a "library," the volumes of which are represented by over 1,800 hams, hanging in tight rows in the house of a certain Monsieur Leblanc of Paris. As we see, things have hardly changed in France as far as *cochonailles* are concerned. We could translate this word by "porkeries" if it existed. It covers all the preserved pork products, salted, dried, smoked, or cooked in pâtés. It has played an important role in the diets of both city and country dwellers, and indeed still does.

Luncheon with ham, or, *The musicians at the table of Michel Richard Delalande,* attributed to R. Levrac de Tournières (1667–1752); MUSEE LAMBINET, VERSAILLES Austin de Croze, who wrote *Les Plats Regionaux de France* in 1928, considered the hams from Artigues-de-Lussac to be of the most superior quality. Cooked, not smoked, they were traditionally fried with garlic and vinegar. They were left in the vinegar for twenty-four hours and served very cold.

Lunch on the grass, Claude Monet
(1840–1926); MUSEE D'ORSAY, PARIS

On the butcher's stall there was also mutton and beef, yearling and veal. Mutton was mainly eaten in summer, beef in winter, and lamb in spring. Doctors in the medieval and Renaissance periods recommended young, tender meats for nobles and members of the leisured classes, those with delicate constitutions. The ordinary people, and those who did hard physical work, were obliged to eat the coarse meats such as mutton, beef, or cow meat, because such heavier and less digestible meats were considered more nourishing.

As time went on and livestock-raising practices improved towards the end of the sixteenth century, the quality of the meat also improved. In the towns consumption continued to increase to the point where, on the eve of the Revolution, Parisians were eating

130–180 lb (60–80 kg) per person per year, compared to barely 65 lb (30 kg) today. Rabelais, writing at the peak of the Renaissance, informs us that people liked their meat well cooked; it was out of the question to eat meat that was still red.

Meats were often parboiled before roasting. Poultry and roasts to be cooked on the spit were precooked in stock, which made them more tender. Meat was boiled or stewed, roasted or broiled (grilled), served with sauces and other accompaniments. It was always the principal element in the middle course of a meal. From the seventeenth and eighteenth centuries, as the *grande cuisine* progressed, carving became more precise. It was at this time that clear distinctions were made between cuts for roasting and broiling (grilling), cuts for braising and boiling, and a definite hierarchy of the different parts of the carcass was set up. The social differentiation between the coarse meats and the more delicate meats of poultry and young animals disappeared, once the important creators of classical cuisine developed a taste for red meats and meats with a hearty flavor, a taste evident on aristocratic tables.

Refrigeration was an important development, discovered and perfected during the second half of the nineteenth century by two Frenchmen, Ferdinand Carré and Charles Tellier. At first restricted to hotels and professional kitchens, refrigerators have since

The meat-day meal, Jean Baptiste Siméon Chardin (1699–1779); THE LOUVRE, PARIS This is a companion piece to *The fast-day meal*, which also features a collection of utensils but has herrings hanging up in place of meat. The works simply reflect the religious observances stated in their titles.

Richly decorated book of hours of the duc de Berry: November, The Limbourg Brothers (early fifteenth century);

The three brothers became court painters to the duc de Berry in 1411. Of all his extraordinarily fine collection of manuscripts, this series of illuminated miniatures is the most splendid. It is an example of the International Gothic style, characterized in part by careful attention to details, particularly of landscape, animals, and costume.

become commonplace, so that by the second half of the twentieth century people were eating much less of the meats preserved by salting, drying, or cooking in fat. These traditional products have now become specific ingredients of regional cuisines, or, like the various charcuterie products, gourmet specialties: Bayonne ham, sweet-smelling and lightly salted; the more robust ham from the provinces of Auvergne; dried salami-style sausages, large and small; salted pork belly which used to be stored over the winter and which now is usually eaten with boiled lentils. *Rillettes*, which are made from pork gently simmered in pork fat, pork pâtés, fresh sausages, and cooked ham are almost daily foods on our tables.

Nothing of the animal is ever wasted, and in France offal has always been eaten, and indeed greatly appreciated. According to *Le Ménagier de Paris* tripe was sold in the streets of the city by merchants, men or women, who carried it in large shallow bowls. It was a food for the poor, inexpensive and nutritious. There were many recipes for tripe, and we have been bequeathed several flavorsome versions, such as the famous *tripes à la mode de Caen*, from the town of Caen, in which the tripe is lengthily simmered in wine with aromatic herbs and vegetables, and the traditional tripe dish from Lyons, *tablier de sapeur* (*sapeur's* apron), so-called because the dish resembled the long apron the *sapeur* wore in the army. (The *sapeurs* were trench and tunnel diggers.) In all, there are more than twenty different recipes. Then we have the famous *andouilles* and *andouillettes* celebrated in the Renaissance by Rabelais. These are strong-tasting sausages made entirely of tripe, flavored with herbs, sometimes smoked like the *andouille de Vire* in Brittany. Brains, kidneys and liver are the favorites among offal, especially calf's liver, a delicate and fortifying food recommended for convalescents and children. Even the blood is eaten, in particular pig's blood, in the form of blood pudding. Regional variations add little chunks of fat or spinach, or flavor it with onions or spices. *Boudin blanc*, or white sausage, is a kind of mousse of white meats inside a sausage skin and is typically associated with Christmas.

Meat consumption may well have varied over the centuries, but French farmers still produce some of the best meats in Europe. Charolais beef cannot be equaled, although Scottish beef comes close. Mutton and lamb from the Lot and the Alps, and the *pré salé* (salt meadow) lamb from Normandy, are particularly delectable. In France the leg of lamb is associated with special meals and Sunday dinners. Veal has always been destined for delicate constitutions — women, aristocrats, and people who are ill; the French prefer it to be very pale and thus from very young animals who have been fed only on milk. Veal has had a prominent place in recipe collections since the seventeenth century. It is always thoroughly cooked and often presented in a sauce, as in the *blanquette de veau*; for this dish the veal is gently simmered in stock, then served in a sauce thickened with egg yolks and cream and seasoned with lemon juice.

Pork and beef account for the greater part of meat consumption, and it would hardly be an exaggeration to say that it has been like this since the time of the Gauls. In addition to the various charcuterie products described previously, there are chops and roasts which occur frequently in the daily diet. Since absolutely nothing of this animal is ever wasted, even the trotters have given rise to a famous dish: pigs trotters *à la Sainte-Menehould*. They are gently cooked, coated in breadcrumbs, then broiled (grilled) and accompanied by a sauce, a style of preparation which is typically medieval. Pigs' ears can be prepared in the same manner.

Finally, mention should be made of a meat that is slowly disappearing from the marketplace, horsemeat. In fact the combined influence of nineteenth-century hygienists and economic pressures led the French to begin to eat horsemeat, said to be more nutritious than beef and a cure for anemia. Doctors recommended eating it raw, thus starting a fashion for tartar steak. Anemic children were taken to the slaughterhouse to drink warm raw horse blood, believed to be a cure for their ailment. In many families in the 1960s the horsemeat steak was a daily event. Today horsemeat butchers and the advocates of horsemeat are becoming more rare, despite articles from the world of medical research recommending horsemeat for its leanness and therefore its suitability for those with cholesterol problems. Having said that, it should also be added that there are no recipes for horsemeat in the important texts of *cuisine classique*.

In recent years meat, particularly red meat, has been losing its traditional importance on our tables. This is not only due to new attitudes towards what the medical world considers a healthy diet, but also to the changes introduced by Nouvelle Cuisine. Young chefs have been successfully exploring less privileged domains, such as seafood and fish, in search of lighter and more unusual tastes. Meat lovers need not worry: like all fashions it will probably pass.

Afternoon nap in the country, Gustave Courbet (1819–77); MUSEE DE LA VILLE DE PARIS, PETIT PALAIS, PARIS
While staying in Le Havre in 1868, Courbet and Monet took it upon themselves to visit Alexandre Dumas, renowned writer and lover of food, whom they had never met. They struck an instant rapport. Gustave Geffroy in his biography *Claude Monet* (1922) records that "when Dumas and Courbet were not talking, they would sing or cook together; Courbet made dishes from his native Franche-Comté, Dumas dishes from the whole world."

155

Beef casseroled with onions (left); Pot-au-feu with three meats and green sauce (right)

BEEF CASSEROLED WITH ONIONS

Daube de boeuf aux oignons   Serves 4

Of all old French kitchen utensils, a venerable cast-iron dish has traditionally held pride of place: *la danbière*, the stewing-pan. In this, on the kitchen stove next to the hearth, succulent meats basted with wine and sprinkled with spices would be left to simmer slowly for hours over a very low flame. The results were delectable stews, which were particularly popular among the bourgeoisie and which for today's French people evoke memories of Grandmother's cooking and of appetizing aromas emanating from dishes lovingly prepared for many hours over cast-iron stoves. This recipe conjures up the same unmistakable flavor and wonderful taste. Stews are a traditional dish throughout the country, but in the South they are served with pasta, whereas in the North they are served with potatoes.

2 lb (1 kg) top rump roast of beef, tied with string
salt and freshly ground pepper
7 whole cloves
2 lb (1 kg) large onions, cut into ½ inch (1 cm) slices
10 oz (315 g) medium spaghetti
½ cup (2 oz/60 g) finely and freshly grated
  Parmesan cheese

Preheat the oven to 250°F (130°C/Gas ½).

Season the meat with salt and pepper, and stick the cloves into the roast. Line the bottom of a 4 qt (4 l) stoneware or cast-iron pot with the onions. Sprinkle with salt. Place the meat on top. Cover the pot and place in the oven. Cook for 5 hours, turning the meat once or twice.

After 5 hours, remove the pot and lift the lid: a delicious aroma will arise from the pot where everything is golden: the inside of the pot, the meat, the onions. Remove the string from the meat.

Set the meat on a serving plate and decorate it with half of the onion rings. Cover the dish with foil or keep it warm in the turned-off oven.

In a pot, bring water to a boil. Add salt and the spaghetti. Cook until *al dente*.

Over a large pan, pass the remaining onions and cooking juices through the medium disk of a food mill.

Drain the spaghetti. Toss with the puréed onions in the pan and cook for 1 minute over low heat. Pour the spaghetti into a deep serving dish.

Serve the beef and the spaghetti at the same time. Sprinkle the spaghetti with Parmesan and pepper just before presenting them with the meat, which will be so tender that you can serve it with a spoon.

POT-AU-FEU WITH THREE MEATS AND GREEN SAUCE

Pot-au-feu aux trois viandes, sauce verte   Serves 6

Pot-au-feu, which consists of broth, boiled meat and vegetables, is the most traditional of all French dishes. Every country in Europe has its own version of boiled meat, but in France it has long been a yardstick by which good cooks are judged. In many provinces, it was the Sunday lunch and the only time that meat was eaten and when the three elements of the dish were put to maximum use, the cold meat leftovers being eaten the following days with onion sauce. Like stews, beef *pot-au-feu* is one of those dishes that strongly conjures up middle-class and peasant cooking traditions.

1¾ lb (800 g) beef: blade roast (chuck, blade), boneless shoulder pot roast (neck, chuck), shank (shin) or brisket
1¼ lb (600 g) lamb shoulder
1¼ lb (600 g) veal shank (nut)
1 large carrot, quartered
1 small onion (2 oz/60 g) stuck with 3 whole cloves
3 garlic cloves
2 teaspoons coarse sea salt
1 teaspoon mixed peppercorns
2 celery ribs (stalks), with their leaves
2 parsley sprigs
1 thyme sprig
1 bay leaf

Vegetables
18 small carrots, peeled
12 small turnips, scraped
the white part of 12 leeks
12 small potatoes, peeled
3 celery hearts

Sauce
1 garlic clove, peeled
leaves of 12 flat-leaf (Italian) parsley sprigs
4 anchovy fillets
8 walnuts, shelled
½ oz (15 g) fresh white breadcrumbs
1 tablespoon drained capers
6 small gherkins
2 shallots, peeled
1 hardboiled egg, peeled and quartered
2 tablespoons wine vinegar
⅓ cup (3 fl oz/90 ml) extra virgin olive oil

Rinse the meats and place them in a large cooking pot. Add the carrot chunks, the clove-studded onion, the whole garlic cloves, and the salt and peppercorns. With kitchen thread, tie together the celery, parsley, thyme and bay leaf. Add cold water to cover. Bring slowly to a boil and then simmer over low heat for 4 to 5 hours, until the meat is very tender. Skim the surface of the liquid during the first 30 minutes.

When the meats are cooked, turn off the heat. Remove the vegetables and spices from the broth. Allow the broth to rest for about 30 minutes, and remove the fat from the surface with a spoon. (If you have time, allow the broth to rest for several hours: no fat will remain suspended in the broth and all of the impurities will have fallen to the bottom of the pot. The broth will be perfectly clear.)

Prepare the vegetables. Add the carrots, turnips, leeks, potatoes and celery hearts to a large pot of boiling salted water. Cook for 10 minutes, and drain. Transfer the vegetables to an 11 inch (28 cm) nonstick skillet and half cover them with the fat-free broth. Cover and cook the vegetables over medium heat for 15 to 20 minutes, until they are tender and there is no more liquid in the pan.

Prepare the green sauce. In a food processor, combine the garlic, parsley, anchovies, nuts, breadcrumbs, capers, gherkins, shallots, hardboiled egg and the vinegar. Slowly add the oil and process until smooth; pour into a sauceboat.

Reheat the broth and the meats. Serve the meats cut in slices and garnished with the vegetables in a bowl. Pour the broth into the bowl and spoon on the sauce.

POACHED TENDERLOIN OF BEEF WITH CELERY AND CHANTERELLES

Boeuf à la ficelle, céleri et chanterelles   Serves 4

For a long time the French scorned English cooking because, they said, everything was boiled, not realizing that this basic cooking technique is also part of their own tradition. This delicious dish demonstrates to what extent this type of cooking allows seemingly simple preparations to be extraordinarily refined as well. This is, of course, partly due to the flavor of the wild mushrooms, which can never be equaled by humble cultivated mushrooms.

4 thick slices of boneless beef: tenderloin, filet
   mignon (fillet) or sirloin, 5 oz (155 g) each cut
   1½ inches (3.75 cm) thick
13 oz (410 g) small chanterelles *(wild mushrooms)*
   (see note below)

1 tablespoon coarse sea salt
1 tablespoon black peppercorns
green leaves of 4 celery ribs (stalks)
2 tablespoons (1 oz/30 g) butter
1 small shallot, minced
salt
1½ tablespoons sweet muscat wine
¼ cup (2 fl oz/60 ml) light (single) cream
3 tablespoons chopped tender yellow leaves of
   1 celery heart

Tie kitchen string around each slice of beef in the shape of a cross, forming a 2½ inch (6.25 cm) bow at the center. Trim any hard parts from the *chanterelle* stems, but keep the mushrooms whole. Wash them quickly and pat dry.

Boil water in a 4 qt (4 l) pot. Add the coarse sea salt, peppercorns, and the green celery leaves.

Meanwhile, melt the butter in a 10¼ inch

Poached tenderloin of beef with celery and chanterelles

(26 cm) nonstick skillet. Add the shallot and cook over low heat for 3 minutes, until soft but not golden. Add the *chanterelles* and cook, stirring constantly, over high heat for 5 minutes, until they no longer release water. Season with salt and add the wine. Cook until the wine evaporates. Add the cream and cook for 2 minutes: the cream will reduce and turn light brown. Remove from the heat.

Slip the string bows of the tied slices of beef over the handle of a wooden spoon. Rest the wooden spoon across the pot, with the meat suspended in the simmering seasoned water. The beef will cook perfectly. Allow 4 minutes to obtain rare meat. Remove the beef from the pot and place each piece on a warm plate.

Add the chopped yellow celery leaves to the mushrooms and heat for 30 seconds, stirring. Garnish the meat with the mushrooms and serve immediately.

Note: The *chanterelles* can be replaced by other wild mushrooms: small flap mushrooms cut into thin slices, *pleurotes*, St George's agaric mushrooms, *trompettes de la mort* — or a mixture of many kinds of mushrooms.

HERBED AND SPICY STEAK TARTARE

Tartare aux épices et aux herbes   Serves 4–5

According to legend, invading barbarians such as the Huns, Tartars and other Attilas who marched upon the East of France several thousand years ago, ate pieces of raw meat that they had tenderized by leaving them for a few hours under the horse's saddle. From this legend comes the name "Tartare Steak" given to any ground raw meat dish. The following version is lighter than the traditional recipe, which blends the mixture with an egg yolk.

2 teaspoons Dijon mustard
2 teaspoons French mustard
2 tablespoons lemon juice
2 tablespoons heavy (double) cream
2 tablespoons extra virgin olive oil
2 teaspoons Cognac
⅓ teaspoon ground cumin
⅓ teaspoon ground cayenne pepper
¾ teaspoon fine sea salt
½ teaspoon freshly ground black pepper
6 tablespoons chopped flat-leaf (Italian) parsley

Herbed and spicy steak tartare

1 tablespoon chopped basil (see note below)
2 tablespoons chopped chives
1½ lb (750 g) chilled ground (minced) beef

Mix the 2 mustards in a large bowl. Add the lemon juice, cream, oil, Cognac, cumin, cayenne, salt and pepper. Mix well, and then add the parsley, basil and chives. Add the ground beef and mix thoroughly with two forks, aerating the mixture rather than squashing it or turning it.

Mound the tartare onto serving dishes and serve immediately, with various salads and toasted bread, or with Potato Cakes (p.196).

Note: The basil may be replaced by tarragon, chervil, dill or fresh coriander (cilantro).

ROAST BEEF IN PEPPER CRUST

Rôti de boeuf en croûte de poivres   Serves 4

The French word *rosbif* has, of course, come from the English. It simply means "roast beef," which the French eat rare and like very tender. About thirty years ago, before such revolutionary chefs as Michel Guérard brought a breath of fresh air to French cuisine, the traditional meal cooked for guests of middle-class people was *rosbif* served with green beans — no doubt excellent, but lacking in variety! In this recipe, the pepper crust yields a delightful aroma and adds wonderful flavor to the meat.

*1¾ lb (800 g) tenderloin (rump roast), about
    2¼ inches (6 cm) in diameter, tied with string*
1 teaspoon black peppercorns
1 teaspoon white peppercorns
1 teaspoon green peppercorns in brine
1 teaspoon coarse sea salt
1 teaspoon dried thyme leaves
½ teaspoon peanut (groundnut) oil

Allow the meat to stand at room temperature for 1 hour before you cook it.

Preheat the oven to 475°F (240°C/Gas 9). Place a cast-iron or porcelain baking dish or roasting pan large enough for the roast in the oven to preheat.

Combine the 3 types of peppercorns with the coarse salt in a mortar. Grind together, and add the thyme; mix well.

Pat the roast dry and brush it with the oil. Season evenly with the ground herbs and spices.

Place a rack in the baking dish so that the meat will be exposed to heat on all sides. Place the meat on the rack and cook for 30 minutes. Turn off the oven, and let the roast rest in the oven for another 10 minutes without opening the oven door.

Slice the roast ½ inch (1 cm) thick; the slices will be cooked pink throughout. Arrange on a warm plate and serve with Mashed Potatoes (p. 196) garnished with thyme.

This roast is also delicious served cold. Remove it from the oven after the 10 minutes of resting time and let it cool on a rack so that the meat is not bathed in its own juices — however little there may be. Serve in very thin slices, with salad, fresh onions and olives.

STEWED LOIN OF VEAL

Longe de veau en ragoût   Serves 6

This recipe appears in *La Maison Rustique*, which was published in 1745. Since the Middle Ages, veal has been considered, like poultry, a meat for aristocrats, and for people of weak health. It was regarded as more disgestible and finer than beef or other red meats. This idea of refinement and digestibility has lasted to our day, and it retains the image of a luxury meat.

> It must be larded with large cubes of pork fat and seasoned with salt and pepper; you cook it on the spit, and when it is almost cooked you remove it and put it in a pan with broth, a glass of white wine, a bouquet of herbs, mushrooms, morels; and *mousserons* [a kind of wild mushroom], artichoke bases, asparagus, according to the season; then add the drippings from the veal and a little flour, let everything simmer until the sauce is well reduced, then arrange it in a dish and serve very hot.

1 thick veal steak, about 2½ lb (1.2 kg)
salt
1 tablespoon peanut (groundnut) oil
3 tablespoons (1½ oz/45 g) butter
4 shallots, minced
¼ cup (2 fl oz/60 ml) dry white vermouth
⅓ cup (3 fl oz/90 ml) dry white wine

Roast beef in pepper crust

24 thin green asparagus spears

4 artichoke hearts

6½ oz (200 g) small wild mushrooms, such as mousserons (small edible mushrooms), or morels

⅓ cup (3 fl oz/90 ml) chicken broth (stock)

Season the veal with salt.

Heat the oil in an oval casserole. Add 2 table-spoons of the butter and heat until melted. Add the veal and shallots and brown on all sides over low heat, about 15 minutes; the outside of the veal should be lightly caramelized.

Pour the vermouth into the pot and cook until it evaporates. Pour in the wine and cook, covered, over low heat for 1 hour. Turn the meat frequently.

Meanwhile, prepare the vegetables. Cut the asparagus tips into 2¾ inch (7 cm) lengths; reserve the stalks for another use. Quarter the artichoke hearts, then cut each quarter into 3 thin strips. Rinse the mushrooms and wipe dry.

After cooking the meat for 1½ hours, pour the broth into the pot and add the vegetables. Cook for 20 minutes, turning the meat and vegetables once. When the meat and vegetables are tender, remove from the pot and keep warm.

Boil the cooking juices until very thick. Whisk in the remaining butter; the sauce will be very thick and golden.

Slice the roast and arrange on a plate. Garnish with the vegetables, blanket with the sauce and serve.

Stewed loin of veal

163

Blanquette de veau (left); Stuffed veal (right)

BLANQUETTE DE VEAU

Blanquette de veau   Serves 4

This type of dish, more typical of the middle class than the nobility, first appeared in the eighteenth century, along with the thickening of sauces with flour and cream. In the nineteenth century, sauces were thickened with cream and an egg, and at the end of the cooking, separately sautéed onions and mushrooms were added. We prefer thickening with cream alone, as this is lighter. And we add a touch of vanilla. Untraceable by taste, it makes the sauce even more sensuous.

This most traditional of dishes in French cuisine has not changed substantially since the eighteenth century: it is all there, meat carefully boiled, velvety sauce, cream, lemon juice etc. It is an outstanding dish that requires skill to achieve the perfect consistency, and is an excellent example of some techniques of *grande cuisine*.

1½ lb (750 g) veal shoulder, cut into 1 inch (2.5 cm) cubes
1 lb (500 g) veal breast, sliced ½ inch (1 cm) thick
2 cups (16 fl oz/500 ml) chicken broth (stock)
3 carrots, sliced ¼ inch (5 mm) thick
4 tender celery leaves
1 small shallot, minced
1 small onion, minced
1 garlic clove, peeled
salt and freshly ground pepper
½ cup (4 fl oz/125 ml) thick crème fraîche
¼ teaspoon vanilla extract (essence)
2 teaspoons lemon juice

Boil water in a large pot and immerse the pieces of meat. Boil for 1 minute; drain and rinse the meat under cold water: this way, you will make a very clear broth,

164

Pour the broth into a 5 qt (5 l) pot. Add 2 cups (16 fl oz/500 ml) water and bring to a boil. Add the carrots, celery leaves, shallot, onions and garlic, salt and pepper. Cover the pot and simmer for 1 hour 40 minutes.

Pour the contents of the pot through a strainer set over a large saucepan. Discard the garlic and return the meat and vegetables to the cooking pot. Boil the cooking liquid in the saucepan until reduced to ¾ cup (6 fl oz/185 ml). Whisk in the *crème fraîche*, vanilla extract and lemon juice and continue whisking for 1 minute.

Pour the thickened and flavored sauce over the meat, and warm for 5 minutes over very low heat. Serve at once with fresh tagliatelle garnished with sage.

STUFFED VEAL

Paupiettes de veau   Serves 4

For at least three centuries, these thin, stuffed cutlets (escalopes, schnitzels) have been part of our culinary heritage. Together with beef Bourguignonne and beef with carrots, they occupied a prominent place on the menu of popular restaurants between the two world wars. For the young of today, they are one of "Grandma's dishes" — which does not detract in any way from their exquisite taste.

8 very thin veal cutlets (escalopes, schnitzels), about 2¾ oz (80 g) each, pounded very thin

salt and freshly ground pepper

1 oz (30 g) fresh brioche crumbs

2½ tablespoons (1 fl oz/30 ml) milk

Cognac

3 tablespoons (1½ oz/45 g) butter

5 oz (155 g) small cultivated mushrooms, finely chopped

2 shallots, minced

3½ oz (100 g) cooked ham, coarsely chopped

2½ oz (75 g) raw ham, coarsely chopped

6 walnuts, shelled and coarsely chopped

1 tablespoon chopped flat-leaf (Italian) parsley

1 teaspoon chopped tarragon

4 pinches grated nutmeg

1½ oz (45 g) grated Emmenthal cheese

1 egg

1 tablespoon dry white vermouth

1 tablespoon port or Madeira wine

½ cup (4 fl oz/125 ml) thick crème fraîche

Season the veal lightly with salt and pepper on both sides.

Prepare the stuffing. In a bowl, combine the brioche crumbs, milk and Cognac.

Melt 1 tablespoon of the butter in an 8½ inch (22 cm) nonstick skillet. Add the mushrooms and stir over high heat for 3 minutes until lightly golden. Add the shallots and cook for 1 minute. Add the 2 types of ham and the nuts. Cook for 1 minute. Pour the mixture into a bowl and add the parsley, tarragon, soaked brioche crumbs, nutmeg, Emmenthal cheese, and salt and pepper to taste. Break the egg into the bowl and mix well.

Fill each slice of veal with one-eighth of the stuffing. Roll the meat around the stuffing and tie with white thread.

Cook the veal. Melt the remaining 2 tablespoons of butter in a 10¼ inch (26 cm) nonstick skillet. Add the veal rolls and cook for 10 minutes, until browned on all sides. Add the vermouth and cook until evaporated. Add 2 tablespoons water. Cover and cook over gentle heat for 45 minutes, turning the rolls at regular intervals.

Remove the veal rolls and keep warm between 2 dishes. Pour in the Madeira and scrape the pan until the sauce is thick and syrupy. Stir in the *crème fraîche* and meat juices and cook until the sauce becomes velvety thick. Return the meat to the pan and warm it for 2 minutes over gentle heat. Arrange the veal in a deep dish, blanket with the sauce and serve with fresh pasta or brown rice garnished with oregano.

Cooks preparing meat in a pot, tapestry by Queen Mathilde (*circa* 1080); BAYEUX CATHEDRAL

LEG OF LAMB WITH PURÉED GARLIC

Gigot d'agneau à la purée d'ail   Serves 6

On French tables, a leg of lamb is by far the most popular choice for the Sunday roast. One of the most popular breeds of lamb is that from Haute Provence and Normandy, called *pré-salé*. The name means "of salted meadows," due to the fact that they graze in meadows beside the sea, which gives a delicate salty taste to their meat. The French prefer lamb to mutton, which to them tastes too strong. Garlic is a traditional and indispensable complement to lamb.

20 large young garlic cloves
½ tablespoon rosemary leaves
½ tablespoon thyme leaves
salt and freshly ground pepper
1 trimmed leg of lamb, about 3½ lb (1.7 kg)
2 tablespoons peanut (groundnut) oil

Preheat the oven to 475°F (240°C/Gas 9).

Peel the outer layers of the garlic cloves, but leave the last layer: so you have garlic cloves in jackets. Peel 1 of these cloves and cut it into 6 strips. In a bowl, combine the rosemary, thyme, ½ teaspoon fine salt and milled pepper. Roll the strips of garlic in this mixture.

Pierce the leg of lamb in 6 places with the point of a knife and slide the spiced garlic strip in each slit. Lightly oil the leg and season it with the rest of the seasoning mixture in the bowl.

Oil a big enamel plate or roasting pan, place a rack inside and put the lamb, flat side up, on the rack. Oil the garlic cloves in their jackets and slide them onto the plate, under the lamb.

Put the plate in the oven and cook for 25 minutes. Turn the leg, reduce the temperature to 475°F (240°C/Gas 9) and cook for 25 minutes. Watch the garlic cloves and turn them. Be sure that their juices do not burn; they must only caramelize. If the garlic begins to brown too much, add a few tablespoons of hot water from time to time.

After 50 minutes of cooking, a leg of this weight is cooked rare. Turn it and let stand for 10 minutes in the turned-off oven.

At serving time, discard the cooking fat in the plate. Add 2 to 3 tablespoons of water to the plate if the juice is caramelized, then pour this sauce in a sauceboat. Add the mashed pulp of 2 of the roasted garlic cloves.

Put the leg on a serving platter and surround it with the garlic cloves in jackets: each guest will lightly mash the cloves to recover the pulp and eat it with the meat or spread it on slices of toasted bread.

Serve with Tian of Zucchini, Tomatoes and Onions (p.198).

The ham, Paul Gauguin (1848–1903); THE PHILLIPS COLLECTION, WASHINGTON DC

Leg of lamb with puréed garlic

VEGETABLES

Reading the earliest collections of French recipes, one gets the impression that they related to a society in which vegetables were almost completely absent from the diet. Since the early Middle Ages vegetables have not had a good reputation from the viewpoint of doctors, who considered them to have little nutritional value compared with meat or bread. In their dietetic precepts they advised people to stick to hazelnuts, almonds, figs, grapes, melons, and cherries — which had to be eaten at the beginning of the meal so as not to disturb the digestion of the "real" foods, of animal origin. From this long-ago era we have retained the habit of starting a meal with melon.

But to whom did the Faculty of Medicine address its advice during these centuries? To the aristocrats and nobles, the wealthy and well-born, the prosperous bourgeois. Fruits and vegetables had different social values. At the limit, fruits such as those mentioned above could be included in an aristocratic diet, but green and leafy vegetables and roots were strictly for the poor and peasants, those lower down on the social scale. In fact these products of the garden, together with cereals, were without doubt the main foods of the peasants. They would munch their onion and garlic with a hunk of bread, and their soup of cabbage and herbs would be waiting on the hearth after a day's work. Their standard diet could be varied with peas, broad beans, or other legumes. Nevertheless it was not only those who lived in the country who ate legumes in this era. Town-dwellers and craftspeople, monks and friars, made up a substantial population: they ate thick soups made from cabbage, spinach, broad beans, and leeks, enhanced with onions, chickpeas, lentils, turnips, and other root vegetables. If the townspeople did not possess their own vegetable gardens at the back of their houses, they had access to the produce of the market gardeners and farmers on the edge of the town. The monasteries of course were entirely self-sufficient, amply provisioned by their own holdings. The sedate gentleman who wrote *Le Ménagier de Paris* offers several recipes for what he calls *Potages communs sans épices et non lians*, that is, ordinary dishes without spices and unthickened, based on leeks, Swiss chard (silverbeet) or peas, with parsley roots or parsnips. This last-mentioned and tasty vegetable had a long career in French cuisine before disappearing during the nineteenth century. Why did we neglect it, while our English neighbors still appreciate it? Other vegetables, too, have vanished from our kitchens — hyssop and rue, lovage, pennyroyal, shepherd's purse, borage and salad burnet. All these crunchy or aromatic "herbs" survived

Harvesting potatoes, E. Masson (nineteenth century); MUSEE ROUBAIX
In the mid-nineteenth century, at least 75 per cent of France's population still worked on the land. The Romantic artists' depictions of jovial peasants in colorful clothing were in direct contrast to the solemn "realism" of other artists working at this time, notably Millet.

French peasant, Jost Amman, illustration
from *Habitus Praecipuorum Popularum*
(1577); NATIONAL LIBRARY, MADRID
The woman is carrying home a selection
of root vegetables. The radish was not
cultivated in France until the sixteenth
century, while the parsnip was much
enjoyed during the Middle Ages and the
Renaissance.

And the potato, you will ask next? Curiously, the French were suspicious of it. Other European countries adopted it much earlier. Introduced from America in 1540, the potato had become an important peasant food in Germany, Flanders, Switzerland, and Spain by the seventeenth century. But in France it was said that potatoes caused leprosy, that they were good only for pigs. Famine struck in the 1700s, but the French still refused potatoes. It was then that Parmentier intervened. This young pharmacist had been made prisoner at Hanover and had been sustained during a year of captivity by these celebrated tubers. Convinced of the nutritional benefits of the vegetable, he undertook a crusade to have this food accepted by his fellow citizens. One of which, the celebrated Le Grand d'Aussy who wrote *L'Histoire de la Vie Privée des Français*, gave everybody's opinion on the matter: "The doughy taste, the natural insipidity and the unhealthy quality of this indigestible and flatulent food led to its rejection by all delicate households and has been sent back to the people whose rougher palate and more vigorous stomach is satisfied with anything that can appease its hunger." Nevertheless, Parmentier managed to convince the king, Louis XVI, of the strength of his intention, and the latter put at his disposition a field to be planted with potatoes. To excite the curiosity of the public the field was kept under military guard. However, the soldiers had orders to turn a blind eye to the theft of the tubers, if there were people who liked them. The flavor of forbidden fruit ... Then Parmentier offered potato flowers to the King and Queen, who put them in their buttonholes. The trick worked: all the courtiers wanted them. Thus, by a sort of hierarchical route, the humble potato slowly conquered the kitchens, though in France it never reached the importance it acquired in the countries of Northern Europe. During the Revolution, bread was scarce, particularly in cities. It became a republican virtue to eat potatoes in its place. The very first cookbook ever written by a woman in France was published during that period. Its title was *La Cuisinière Républicaine*, and the author, Madame Mérigot, gave recipes only for preparing potatoes. (One could say that this humble tuber has had at least the merit of opening the way for women food writers!)

In the South of France vegetables have always had a more important culinary role than they do in the Northern regions. Tomatoes and fennel, artichokes and cardoons, green beans and broad beans, eggplant (aubergine) and bell peppers (capsicums) were commonly eaten from the end of the 1500s. Two or three centuries had to pass before all these excellent vegetables became part of the ordinary repertoire of cooks north of the Loire. The rest of the country was happy enough with cabbage in all its forms, leeks, spinach, beans, carrots, and peas. Squashes and root vegetables formed the basis of soups and stocks. Garlic and onion were used in often homeopathic doses; in the famous cook book from the beginning of the twentieth century, *La Cuisine de Madame de Saint Ange*, each time that onion or garlic is suggested it is specified that they should be used only if guests can tolerate them, implying that people of delicate taste naturally find these overpowering flavors disgusting. It is through gradual acceptance of Southern recipes that these bulbs have today become indispensable. Until the great changes set in train by Nouvelle Cuisine, the French considered vegetables to be more of a garnish to a dish of meat or fish than a separate food, with the exception of salads, which have an almost therapeutic role after heavy meat dishes to "help the digestion."

The nineteenth century gave vegetables only a secondary role in *grande cuisine*. The beginnings of a change — which was really not felt until the 1970s — came with the first

reformist movements, the utopians and the first vegetarians. Again, it was great cooks such as Michel Guérard who gave vegetables the choice position they deserved, both for our health and well-being, and for the greater pleasures of the table. Today we are gradually rediscovering the forgotten vegetables of which La Quintinie and his followers were so proud: parsnip and "salad greens," an infinite variety of squashes, samphire, and saltwort, the roots of chervil and parsley, and many more. Several garden producers have specialized in the production of "forgotten" or "new" vegetables, herbs and fruit. In a lovely château near Paris, at Saint Jean de Beauregard, there is a yearly exhibit of all these plants. There, you can converse with the squash and pumpkin specialists presenting dozens of varieties, some of which are having immense success, such as the "potimarron," tasting of sweet chestnut and soft pumpkin. There are all kinds of root vegetables, cabbages, and beans. All the ancient herbs are present, and many young cooks are making good use of them, such as adding hyssop to rabbit stews. At the same exhibit you can meet the representatives of a nationwide association called "Les Croqueurs de Pommes" (apple-munchers). They regroup all collectors of ancient varieties of apples, which they cultivate and distribute across the country, bringing back to life fruit which has completely disappeared from the markets, overtaken by the industrial productions such as Golden Delicious or Granny Smith!

The Marché des Innocents in Paris, Tardieu (early nineteenth century); THE LOUVRE, PARIS
Grapes spill from the table of one of the vendors. Used in *pâtisserie,* served with quail and *boudin blanc,* grapes are also made into jams such as *raisiné,* a specialty of Burgundy. The juice is simmered with pieces of a variety of fruits; no sugar is added. Alternatively, the jam may be made using sweet wine.

There are also new trends: young chefs who started to explore the possibilities of fish seem to be rediscovering the sea. All of a sudden, seaweed has entered French cuisine. Gathered fresh and healthy from the rocky coast of Brittany, it is sold by fishmongers to be prepared into salads, steamed with shellfish, sautéed as a vegetable, or used as flavoring for sauces to go with fish. More and more specialty shops offer seaweed-flavored spaghetti or noodles, as well as breads and biscuits — there is even a seaweed jam!

The story of mushrooms, gathered from the fields, begins when they were the food of starving peasants. Mushrooms attracted the interest of cooks and gourmands only from the start of the sixteenth century, and at that time it was only parasol mushrooms and field mushrooms that were eaten. In the seventeenth century mushrooms became very fashionable. Was this perhaps connected with the efforts of La Quintinie, who invented a way of cultivating mushrooms, and Louis XIV's predilection for them? Morels and mousserons were frequently mentioned in *La Cuisinière Bourgeoise* (1774) and gradually a kind of culinary hierarchy was established. First were morels, cèpes and girolles, next the mousserons, the field mushrooms and parasol mushrooms, then the stragglers, lactaries and grisettes and others, and finally right at the bottom the cultivated mushrooms which, it must be admitted, were available year-round but which had very little flavor.

Still life with artichoke, Hippolyte Chaignet (1820–65); MUSEE DES BEAUX-ARTS, DIJON
Lying beside the artichoke is the knobbly root vegetable known as celeriac. Celeriac may be cooked in a purée with potato, or shredded and marinated in a mustardy French dressing to make an *hors d'oeuvre*.

The mysterious, perfumed black truffle has not always been part of the French culinary domain. Hardly mentioned, if at all, before the sixteenth century, it used to be cooked in a very peculiar way: in wine with vinegar, salt, and pepper (*Le Cuisinier François*), or boiled in a spiced stock. Neither method could highlight the magnificent flavor of this fungus. From the seventeenth century it was recognized that the best truffles came from the Périgord, where they were harvested with the aid of a pig whose keen sense of smell allowed it to pinpoint the spot where the truffle was buried. There were also truffles in Provence, where dogs were preferred for the search (they were less greedy than pigs). Little by little truffles acquired an enormous prestige and became essential ingredients in numerous recipes. Towards the middle of the nineteenth century, along with crayfish, lobster, and *foie gras*, they symbolized the cuisine of the wealthy, luxurious, and sophisticated. Today the important truffle markets take place in winter in the mountain regions of Provence and in the Périgord. This is the best time to eat them, when they are absolutely fresh — raw, thinly sliced, and drizzled with a little olive oil. Nouvelle Cuisine has revalued the truffle which previously had been a fundamental ingredient of sauces and stuffings; now it is the central element on which the dish is built.

Still life with onions, Paul Cézanne (1839–1906); MUSEE D'ORSAY, PARIS
The name Soubise is given to dishes which contain either an onion sauce on a *béchamel* base, or an onion purée thickened with rice. The term was bestowed in honor of the eighteenth-century aristocrat and food lover, Charles de Rohan, Prince of Soubise.

Carrots browned with garlic (left); Swiss chard with anchovies (right)

CARROTS BROWNED WITH GARLIC

Carottes dorées à l'ail   Serves 3

Coming from Spain and Sicily via Italy, the carrot spread through Europe in the fourteenth century. In very old recipe books it is known simply as one of the "roots," and not until the eighteenth century was it considered sufficiently "noble" to become an ingredient in the French *grande cuisine*. A popular peasant food (like most root vegetables), the carrot was almost always present in rural dishes. But this humble vegetable can be exquisite when prepared, for example, in the following way.

2 tablespoons extra virgin olive oil
1 ¼ lb (600 g) baby carrots, sliced diagonally,
  ½ inch (1 cm) thick

12 garlic cloves, halved
salt and freshly ground pepper
1 thyme sprig, leaves minced
1 rosemary sprig, leaves minced

Heat the oil in a 9½ inch (24 cm) nonstick skillet. Add the carrots and garlic and brown for 15 minutes over gentle heat, stirring from time to time.

Season with salt and pepper. Add the thyme and rosemary and cook, stirring now and then, for another 15 minutes.

Remove the carrots and the garlic to a serving plate. They should not have absorbed the oil, and will be crunchy on the outside and soft on the inside.

Serve with pan-fried fish, white meats and roasted poultry.

SWISS CHARD WITH ANCHOVIES

Côtes de blettes aux anchois   Serves 3–4

As long ago as the fourteenth century, the author of *Le Ménagier de Paris* grew Swiss chard (silverbeet) in his garden. This recipe with a southern flavor is one of the best uses for this delicate vegetable.

1¼ lb (600 g) baby Swiss chard (silverbeet)
2 tablespoons extra virgin olive oil
1 fresh hot red chili pepper, minced
2 garlic cloves, halved
6 anchovy fillets in oil, drained and diced

Wash and trim the chard. Cut the leaves diagonally in ½ x 2 inch (1 x 5 cm) strips, removing the fibers. Rinse but do not drain completely.

Heat the oil in a 10¼ inch (26 cm) nonstick skillet. Add the chili pepper and garlic. When the garlic cloves are very lightly browned, remove from the pan. Add the Swiss chard and stir to coat with the oil. Cook, covered, over low heat for about 17 minutes, or until the chard is lightly browned and all of the water has evaporated.

Add the anchovy fillets and cook, uncovered, over very low heat for 3 minutes, or until the anchovies disintegrate.

Serve hot or warm.

This dish is an excellent accompaniment to pan-fried fish and grilled or roasted white meats.

CREAMED BELGIAN ENDIVES

Endives à la crème   Serves 3

Belgian endives (witloof) come from a plant called chicory, which is also the source of numerous varieties grown for salads, such as curly lettuce or escarole. Belgian endive, as we know it, is a fairly recent invention, since it was first produced in the 1860s in Belgium, by an employee of the Brussels Botanical Gardens. It was introduced into France in 1873 and today the northern part of the country is the world's largest producer, even ahead of Belgium. Raw or cooked, this slightly bitter vegetable goes very well with white meats and fish.

1 lb (500 g) Belgian endive (chicory, witloof)
1 tablespoon (½ oz/15 g) butter
salt

1 teaspoon superfine (caster) sugar
2 pinches ground cloves
2 pinches grated nutmeg
1 tablespoon lemon juice
1 tablespoon dark rum
⅓ cup (3 fl oz/90 ml) heavy (double) cream

Cut the endive diagonally into rounds ¼ inch (5 mm) thick, starting at the point and turning them ½ inch (1 cm) at each new cut. At the end of the cutting, only the core remains in the shape of a cone; discard it.

Melt the butter in a 4 qt (4 l) cast-iron skillet. Add the endive and cook, turning it continuously, for 1 minute. Sprinkle with salt, sugar, cloves and nutmeg. Stir in the lemon juice. Add the rum and cook for 1 minute over high heat to evaporate the alcohol. Stir in the cream. Cover and cook over low heat for 25 minutes, stirring from time to time. Serve hot garnished with nutmeg and sprigs of tarragon.

This dish can accompany white fish fillets, scallops and pan-fried veal liver, as well as stewed white meats.

Creamed Belgian endives

Grilled mixed bell peppers (left); Celeriac snowball (right)

GRILLED MIXED BELL PEPPERS

Poivrons grillés panachés   Serves 6

Bell peppers (capsicums) are a relatively new ingredient in our cookbooks. Only since the Second World War have they been treated seriously as a vegetable useful for cooking in ways other than the traditional pickling in vinegar.

Of American origin and members of the same family as chili peppers, bell peppers were first used, from the eighteenth century onwards, in the cuisine of the South of France, particularly in the Provence area, but for a long time did not gain much importance. They started their culinary career much earlier in Italy, in Spain, in Romania and, of course, in Hungary, where it is a relative of the famous paprika. Today bell peppers are a frequent ingredient in modern cuisine.

2 red bell peppers (capsicums), about 8 oz (250 g) each

2 yellow bell peppers (capsicums), about 8 oz (250 g) each

2 green bell peppers (capsicums), about 8 oz (250 g) each

4 baby garlic cloves, finely sliced

⅓ cup (3 fl oz/90 ml) extra virgin olive oil

salt

Broil the bell peppers under a broiler (grill) or on a barbecue grill until the skin is dark. (They must not be burnt as they would then acquire a bitter taste.) The cooking should take about 30 minutes. Place the peppers in a covered pot and let cool for 15 to 20 minutes.

Peel the bell peppers and halve them. If they contain any liquid, save it in a bowl. Discard the ribs and seeds. Cut lengthwise into ¾ inch (2 cm) strips; add to the bowl.

Add the garlic, oil and a little salt; mix well.

Serve immediately while still warm, or else let soak in the refrigerator for a few hours. You can keep these bell peppers for 48 hours, but remove the garlic after 12 hours.

Serve with Eggs Mimosa with Tuna Mousse (p.66), tomato salad, Eggplant (aubergine) Purée (p.195), anchovy fillets, olives or mozzarella. These peppers can also be served with fish and cold meats.

CELERIAC SNOWBALL

Neige de céleri boule   Serves 5–6

Celeriac, or celery root, is also part of the rustic category of "roots," peasant or country food. It was not until the advent of traditional cuisine that vegetables were given greater consideration. Frequently eaten with a *rémoulade* sauce (that is, raw or barely blanched and with a sort of mayonnaise sauce), it is also excellent cooked, as a finely flavored purée.

2 lb (1 kg) celeriac (celery root)
salt
½ cup (4 fl oz/125 ml) thick crème fraîche
2 tablespoons extra virgin olive oil

Bring water to a boil in the lower part of a steamer. Peel the celeriac, wash it and cut into 2 inch (4 cm) cubes. Place in the top of the steamer and sprinkle with salt. Cover and steam for about 35 minutes, until the celeriac is very soft and easily pierced with the point of a knife.

Drain the celeriac in a strainer and let cool. Transfer to a food processor and blend till puréed. Add the *crème fraîche* and mix until the purée is smooth and very white. Add the oil in a thin stream, continuing to process.

Reheat the purée over gentle heat in a double-boiler, steamer or, better still, in a microwave oven. Serve immediately.

This purée is served with poultry — chicken, turkey and duck — either stuffed or not, and roasted. It goes very well with chestnuts and both are delicious blanketed with the juices of the poultry.

The watering-trough, Maître aux Béguins (seventeenth century); THE LOUVRE, PARIS

The gleaners are called home, J. Breton (1827–1906); MUSÉE D'ORSAY, PARIS   Jean-François Millet painted his famous work *The Gleaners* in 1857. The stooped figures of women

eaning quickly became a cliché of peasant paintings during the nineteenth century.

A basket of plums and a basket of strawberries, Louise Moillon (1616–*circa* 1674); MUSEE DES AUGUSTINS, TOULOUSE **The finest still-life painter of the French seventeenth century**

...illon combined intense observation with a mesmerizing sense of stillness. She is noted for her exquisite rendering of the texture of fruit.

Basket of fruit and a small basket of strawberries, LOUISE MOILLON (1616–*circa* 1674); MUSEE DES AUGUSTINS, TOULOUSE

FIG TART WITH BLACKCURRANT JELLY

Tartelettes feuilletées aux   Serves 6
figues, coulis de cassis

The fig comes from the South of France. That great letter-writer, the Marquise de Sévigné (1626–96), when visiting her daughter in her Drôme castle, used to tell her friends: "It is a strange thing about melons, figs and muscat grapes: if we wanted, by some odd fancy, a bad melon, we would have to have it brought from Paris as there are none to be found here." This is true even today; the best figs are those eaten straight from the tree, still warmed by the sun, full of juice and ready to burst. Another excellent way of eating them is to make tarts like this one.

6½ oz (200 g) puff pastry
6 large purple figs, just ripe
2 oz (60 g) finely ground almonds
3 tablespoons (1½ oz/45 g) butter
¼ cup (2 oz/60 g) sugar
1 egg

For the jelly sauce:
1½ cups (6½ oz/200 g) blackcurrants
⅓ cup (3 oz/90 g) superfine (caster) sugar

Prepare the blackcurrant sauce: wash the blackcurrants, stalk them and place them in the food processor. Add the sugar and mix until it becomes a fine purée. Filter it through a fine sieve in order to obtain a thin juice. Reserve.

Set the oven thermostat to 400°F (200°C/Gas 6). Prepare the almond cream: melt the butter and let it cool. Beat the egg in a terrine adding the sugar. Add the finely ground almonds and the butter and mix. Spread the pastry with a rolling pin to ⅛ inch (3 mm) thickness and cut out 6 circles, 4 inch (10 cm) in diameter. Place them on a nonstick tray. Fill with the almond cream.

Cut the figs into 8 pieces and garnish the tarts. Place in the oven and cook for 25 minutes, until the tarts are golden. Remove the tarts from the oven and place them in 6 dishes. Garnish them with the sauce and serve immediately.

APRICOT SHORT-BREAD TARTS

Tartelettes sablées aux abricots   Serves 6

The apricot, like the almond, is an important ingredient in French patisserie-making. In fact this fruit comes from afar and was cultivated by the Chinese 5000 years ago. Gradually, it made its way to the Middle, then Near East, and set its roots in the dry lands of the South of France. The best apricots come from the Roussillon area. As a fresh fruit, it is used in the making of tarts or side-dishes, such as rice *à la Conde* (molded rice pudding with apricots); and as a jam it is used for glazing various pastries.

DESSERTS

pillon combined intense observation with a mesmerizing sense of stillness. She is noted for her exquisite rendering of the texture of fruit.

DESSERTS

In France cheese is served before dessert. Since the adoption of *service à la russe* the meal sequence includes one last savory note before the end. France has nearly 300 different cheeses, in an infinite variety of tastes and textures — cheeses made from goat's, cow's, or sheep's milk, of different shapes and aromas, varying according to the province of origin. There are soft, creamy cheeses, skillfully made, from Normandy, Brie, and other Eastern regions; dry, fresh, or well-matured goat cheeses, and ash-covered ones, from the Center, South, and Southwest; Roquefort from the mountainous Causses, and sheep's milk cheese from the Pyrénées; the cooked cheeses of the Alps; the subtle products of Auvergne. The list is endless. There is a cheese for every taste. In formal banquets, however, from the eighteenth century to the first quarter of the present century the rule was that cheese was never offered to ladies: the aroma and virility of this dish would obviously offend their refined sensibility.

In ordinary homes, daily meals often ended with cheese, and a reminder of this can be seen on certain menus of popular restaurants, where it is specified: cheese *or* dessert.

Dessert, as we know it today, has been the standard ending to a meal for only 150 or so years. Before that time, in the *service à la française* sweet dishes could be offered as part of any *service*, not only at its close. Certain medieval meals, however, as illustrated by the menus suggested in *Le Ménagier de Paris*, written around 1390, conclude with the *issue de table* which was not very different from our idea of dessert. The *issue* was presented to the guests once the tablecloth had been removed; it included the hippocras, a sweetened and spiced wine, and wafers, sometimes accompanied by hazelnuts and almonds, or fresh or dried fruits. If the banquet were a prestigious one, there would also be *dragées*, or *comfits*, which at that time meant aniseed, or other spices, coated with sugar.

Honey was the main sweetener until the end of the Middle Ages. Cane sugar first came to Europe around the eleventh century, brought by the Arabs, who had found it in India. The Indians in turn had obtained the cane from its original area, New Guinea and Indonesia. In the 1400s the Spaniards started cultivating it in the Canary Islands, the Portuguese followed suit in the Azores and Cabo Verde Islands and thus, sugar became more available to European countries. Meanwhile, the crusaders had become familiar with this product in their dealings with the "infidels" of the Near East.

The buffet, Jean Baptiste Siméon Chardin (1699–1779); THE LOUVRE, PARIS
A modest *pièce montée* (set piece) of plums, apples, pears, and peaches. Montreuil, east of Paris, was once famous for its peaches; Louis XIV was sent a basketful every year by a musketeer who lived there, to whom he had granted a pension.

Lemon–raspberry soufflé crêpes

LEMON–RASPBERRY SOUFFLÉ CRÊPES

Crêpes soufflées citron–framboises   Serves 6

In *Le Ménagier de Paris*, written in 1393, this recipe is designated simply *Crespes* (crêpes or pancakes). Crêpes are one of the most ancient ways of cooking paste, a technique derived directly from the making of the first bread loaves. A popular and common delicacy since the Middle Ages, crêpes are eaten traditionally at Candlemas and on Shrove Tuesday. To ensure having money all year, one should turn the pancake over by throwing it in the air with one hand while grasping a gold coin in the other. If the pancake falls back in the pan, wealth is a certainty!

Take flour and mix it with eggs, as many yolks as whites, and dilute it with water, and add salt and wine, and beat it all together well; then melt some fresh pork fat over the fire in a small iron skillet, or use half pork fat half butter, and heat it until it bubbles; and then take a ladle, with a small hole in it, as big as your little finger, and dip the ladle into the mixture, then let the mixture drizzle into the pan, beginning at the middle of the pan and gradually spiralling to the edge; then put it on a plate and sprinkle it with sugar. And the abovementioned skillet, of iron or pewter, should hold three pints (600 ml), and its sides should be half an inch (1 cm) high, and it should be just as wide at the top as at its base, and for good reason.

234

Raspberry sauce

13 oz (410 g) raspberries
⅔ cup (2 oz/60 g) powdered (icing) sugar
1 tablespoon lemon juice

Crêpes

3 tablespoons (1½ oz/45 g) butter
1 cup (8 fl oz/250 ml) milk
2 whole eggs
1 tablespoon rum
1 tablespoon superfine (caster) sugar
¾ cup (3½ oz/100 g) all-purpose (plain) flour

Cooking

2 tablespoons (1 oz/30 g) butter

Lemon soufflé

4 whole eggs, separated
⅓ cup (3 oz/90 g) superfine (caster) sugar
1 tablespoon cornstarch (cornflour)
1 tablespoon lemon juice
grated zest (rind) of 3 lemons
2 eggwhites

Prepare the raspberry sauce. Combine the raspberries, powdered sugar and lemon juice in the bowl of a food processor. Mix at high speed until puréed. Cover and refrigerate.

Prepare the crêpe batter. Melt the butter in a small saucepan over low heat. Add the milk and warm lightly; remove from the heat.

Break the eggs into the container of a blender. Add the rum, sugar, flour and the warmed milk and butter. Blend for 1 minute at low speed; pour the batter into a small bowl.

Since this batter should not be left to stand, cook the pancakes at once: melt the butter in an 8 inch (20 cm) nonstick skillet. Pour off the melted butter into a bowl. Ladle enough batter into the pan to just coat the bottom; lift the pan and move it in a circular motion. After a few seconds of cooking, turn the pancake over with a spatula and cook on the other side for about 10 seconds. When the pancake is cooked, put it on a plate. Prepare 15 of these pancakes — you'll use the 12 best. Between pancakes, lightly butter the pan with a small knotted cloth dipped in the melted butter.

Prepare the lemon soufflé. Beat the egg yolks with half of the sugar until they lighten in color. Add the cornstarch, lemon juice and lemon zest, beating constantly.

Combine all 6 eggwhites in a bowl. Beat until almost stiff and add the rest of the sugar. Beat constantly until the whites are smooth and shiny. Fold one-fourth of the whites into the egg yolk mixture, whipping briskly. Pour this mixture into the whites and fold in gently.

Preheat the oven to 475°F (240°C/Gas 9).

Spread a pancake on a plate and put 2 large tablespoonfuls of the lemon soufflé in the center. Fold the pancake in half, without pressing. Do the same with the other pancakes.

Butter a baking dish capable of containing 12 pancakes set close together. Arrange the pancakes in it. Bake for 4 minutes, until the pancakes open under the pressure of the soufflé that swells as it cooks.

Divide the pancakes among 6 plates and surround them with the raspberry sauce. Eat immediately.

Flowers and fruits, Paul Cézanne (1839–1906); L'ORANGERIE, PARIS

235

Cherry jelly with almonds (bottom); Almond cakes with red fruit (top)

CHERRY JELLY WITH ALMONDS

Soupe de cerises en gelée d'amandes   Serves 4

R ed cherries, once they have been picked off the trees by young maidens and used as earrings, have a limited season. They cannot all be eaten raw and traditionally they have been prepared in all kinds of ways: as jams, as syrup, in tarts, stewed (as in this recipe), or, above all, in their most famous form — brandied cherries. There are numerous varieties of cherries in France, divided into two categories: sweet cherries, which are firm and sweet and originate from the merry-tree or from the European wild cherry tree; and the more sour varieties which produce the best jams and come from a range of wild cherry trees from the Black Sea.

1 lb (500 g) cherries
⅓ cup (3 fl oz/90 ml) cane syrup
2.5 g powdered (1 leaf) unflavored gelatin

24 fresh almonds, shelled, peeled and halved
6 drops natural bitter almond extract (essence)
1 tablespoon Kirsch
2 cups (8 fl oz/250 ml) very cold heavy (double) cream, whipped to form peaks

Wash the cherries, drain and jab each one with a needle a few times to prevent bursting during cooking.

Pour the cane syrup into a big pot and bring to a boil. Sprinkle on the gelatin; it will melt immediately. Bring to a boil. Add the cherries and cook, stirring, for 5 minutes.

Pour the cherries and their juices into a bowl, add almond extract and Kirsch, and set aside to cool. Refrigerate for at least 1 hour.

To serve, divide the cherry jelly among 4 plates. Garnish with the almonds and whipped cream.

236

ALMOND CAKES WITH RED FRUIT

Amandines aux fruits rouges   Serves 8

Almonds and sugar are old companions. In France, they flavor many pastries and desserts: frangipane, marzipan, nougats and many more, including these delicate almond cakes lightened with red fruits.

3½ oz (100 g) finely ground almonds
1 tablespoon potato starch, or 1½ teaspoons cornstarch (cornflour)
4 eggwhites
⅔ cup (5 oz/150 g) superfine (caster) sugar
11 oz (345 g) mixed redcurrants and raspberries
1 tablespoon powdered (icing) sugar

Preheat the oven to 300°F (150°C/Gas 2). Lightly butter eight 3 inch (8 cm) nonstick brioche molds.

Mix the almond powder and the starch. Beat the eggwhites until almost stiff. Add the superfine sugar and beat for 1 minute. Gently fold in the almond–starch mixture. Finally, very gently fold in the redcurrants and raspberries.

Divide the mixture among the molds. Bake for 20 minutes.

Let the small cakes cool for 5 minutes in the molds. Unmold and sprinkle with the powdered sugar. Serve immediately.

If desired, these cakes can be garnished with a cold custard flavored with vanilla or kirsch and made with the 4 unused yolks, 2 cups (16 fl oz/ 500 ml) milk and ⅓ cup (3 oz/90 g) of superfine (caster) sugar.

APPLE TART WITH ALMONDS

Tarte aux pommes aux amandes   Serves 4

This is the original fruit tart. Whether homemade or bought at the bakery or pastry shop, whether based on puff pastry, shortbread or shortcrust pastry, it remains for the French *The Tart*. Over the course of centuries, certain fancy variations have been introduced, such as the *tarte tatin*, which reverses things by putting the apples at the bottom of the mold and the pastry on top.

¾ cup (3½ oz/100 g) all-purpose (plain) flour
¼ cup (2 oz/60 g) butter
1 tablespoon powdered (icing) sugar

6 drops vanilla extract (essence)
2 pinches salt
1¾ oz (50 g) ground almonds
¼ cup (1½ oz/45 g) firmly packed brown sugar
3 pinches ground cinnamon
3 large round yellow apples streaked with russet
2 tablespoons dark rum

Prepare the pastry the night before. Put the flour in the bowl of a food processor. Add the butter, powdered sugar, vanilla powder, salt and 1 tablespoon of water. Mix at high speed for 30 seconds, until the mixture forms a ball. If dough is a little dry, water may be added. Refrigerate the dough in a plastic bag.

The next day, roll out the dough ⅛ inch (3 mm) thick. Line an 8 inch (20 cm) ceramic tart mold with the dough. Place the mold in the refrigerator and let it rest for 1 hour.

After 1 hour, set the oven to 475°F (240°C/ Gas 9).

Make the filling. Combine the ground almonds, brown sugar and cinnamon in a bowl. Quarter the apples, peel and core them. Cut each apple quarter into very thin slices on a nardoline or other thin slicer. Place the slices in a bowl and add the rum. Stir gently.

Remove the mold from the oven and fill the inside of the pastry with the apples. Smooth the surface. Bake for 35 minutes, until golden. Let the tart stand before unmolding it. Serve warm.

Apple tart with almonds

237

Basket of fruit and a small basket of strawberries, LOUISE MOILLON (1616–*circa* 1674); MUSEE DES AUGUSTINS, TOULOUSE

FIG TART WITH BLACKCURRANT JELLY

Tartelettes feuilletées aux figues, coulis de cassis   Serves 6

The fig comes from the South of France. That great letter-writer, the Marquise de Sévigné (1626–96), when visiting her daughter in her Drôme castle, used to tell her friends: "It is a strange thing about melons, figs and muscat grapes: if we wanted, by some odd fancy, a bad melon, we would have to have it brought from Paris as there are none to be found here." This is true even today; the best figs are those eaten straight from the tree, still warmed by the sun, full of juice and ready to burst. Another excellent way of eating them is to make tarts like this one.

6½ oz (200 g) puff pastry
6 large purple figs, just ripe
2 oz (60 g) finely ground almonds
3 tablespoons (1½ oz/45 g) butter
¼ cup (2 oz/60 g) sugar
1 egg

For the jelly sauce:

1½ cups (6½ oz/200 g) blackcurrants
⅓ cup (3 oz/90 g) superfine (caster) sugar

Prepare the blackcurrant sauce: wash the blackcurrants, stalk them and place them in the food processor. Add the sugar and mix until it becomes a fine purée. Filter it through a fine sieve in order to obtain a thin juice. Reserve.

Set the oven thermostat to 400°F (200°C/Gas 6). Prepare the almond cream: melt the butter and let it cool. Beat the egg in a terrine adding the sugar. Add the finely ground almonds and the butter and mix. Spread the pastry with a rolling pin to ⅛ inch (3 mm) thickness and cut out 6 circles, 4 inch (10 cm) in diameter. Place them on a nonstick tray. Fill with the almond cream.

Cut the figs into 8 pieces and garnish the tarts. Place in the oven and cook for 25 minutes, until the tarts are golden. Remove the tarts from the oven and place them in 6 dishes. Garnish them with the sauce and serve immediately.

APRICOT SHORT-BREAD TARTS

Tartelettes sablées aux abricots   Serves 6

The apricot, like the almond, is an important ingredient in French patisserie-making. In fact this fruit comes from afar and was cultivated by the Chinese 5000 years ago. Gradually, it made its way to the Middle, then Near East, and set its roots in the dry lands of the South of France. The best apricots come from the Roussillon area. As a fresh fruit, it is used in the making of tarts or side-dishes, such as rice *à la Conde* (molded rice pudding with apricots); and as a jam it is used for glazing various pastries.

2 cups (8 oz/250 g) all-purpose (plain) flour
10 tablespoons (5 oz/155 g) butter, softened
1¾ oz (50 g) ground hazelnuts
1 cup (2¾ oz/80 g) powdered (icing) sugar
2 eggs
1 pinch salt
2 oz (60 g) ground almonds
3 tablespoons (1½ oz/45 g) butter
¼ cup (1½ oz/45 g) sugar
1 tablespoon Kirsch
24 large ripe apricots
3 tablespoons superfine (caster) sugar

Prepare the pastry: lightly brown the ground hazelnuts in a nonstick skillet over low heat. Let it cool on a dish. Put the butter, sugar, egg, flour and ground hazelnuts in a food processor. Blend at medium speed till it becomes a ball of paste. Let it rest in the refrigerator for 1 hour.

Prepare the almond cream: brown the ground almonds in a nonstick skillet over low heat. Let it cool on a dish. Melt the butter and let it cool. Whisk the egg in a bowl adding the sugar. Add the ground almonds, Kirsch and butter and mix.

Wash the apricots, dry them and cut them into quarters discarding the stones. Place them in a deep dish, skin-side down and sprinkle with sugar. Let them soak.

Set the oven thermostat to 400°F (200°C/Gas 6). Divide the pastry into 6 parts and spread it into 3 inch (8 cm) diameter circles. Using 10 individual tart molds 3 inches (8 cm) in diameter, line the bottoms but not the side with pastry, pushing it with your fingers. Place in the oven and cook for 15 minutes.

After that time, spread a thin layer of almond cream in every pastry mold and return them to the oven. Cook for 20 minutes, then unmold the small tarts and place them on an oven tray.

Turn the broiler (grill) on. Arrange the apricots on the tarts, skin side on the cream, rosette style. Place the tray in the broiler, as close as possible to the heat and let the edges caramelize for about 5 minutes. Remove from the oven and serve at once.

Fig tart with blackcurrant jelly (left); Apricot shortbread tarts (right)

RASPBERRY TART

Clafoutis aux framboises   Serves 4

Clafoutis is an old country dessert traditionally made with unstoned cherries, but there are all kinds of varieties. It is akin to a pancake batter, oven-baked in a mold and garnished with fruit.

1 egg
2 egg yolks
⅔ cup (6 oz/180 g) superfine (caster) sugar
1 tablespoon all-purpose (plain) flour
1 cup (8 fl oz/250 ml) heavy (double) cream
10 oz (315 g) raspberries

Preheat the oven to 375°F (190°C/Gas 5). In a bowl, combine the whole egg, egg yolks and ½ cup (4 oz/125 g) of the sugar. Whisk well, without foaming. Sift the flour on top, add the cream and whisk until well mixed.

Spread the raspberries in an 8½ in (22 cm) ovenproof ceramic tart dish. Sprinkle on the remaining superfine sugar and stir to coat the berries. Gently pour the mixture over the raspberries.

Bake the clafoutis for about 30 minutes, until the tart has set and its surface is golden. Serve warm.

PEARS WITH SAFFRON HONEY

Poires au miel de safran   Serves 6

This contemporary dessert reflects medieval traditions that used saffron for both flavor and color. Pears are a fruit admirably suited to cooking and here, in their saffron syrup, they attain perfection.

Raspberry tart (left); Pears with saffron honey (right)

⅔ cup (5 fl oz/155 ml) acacia honey
6 large pears, such as red Williams
1 lemon, halved
6 pinches saffron threads

Pour the honey into a deep saucepan just large enough to hold the pears upright. Add 3 tablespoons water and bring to a boil.

Peel the pears, leaving their stems intact. Rub the pears with the lemon halves.

Stand the pears upright in the hot syrup and cook over low heat for about 20 minutes, until soft.

Drain the pears and stand them in a fruit dish. Add the saffron to the syrup and set over low heat. Cook until reduced and very syrupy. Coat the pears with the thick syrup.

Serve these pears hot or warm; they are also excellent cold or chilled. Serve with Almond Tuiles (p. 248).

Delectable fritters

DELECTABLE FRITTERS

Beignets-mignons   Makes 24 fritters

This recipe comes from *La Maison Rustique*, published in 1745. Similar to pancakes, these fritters are a very old delicacy, and are made particularly for Shrove Tuesday and Candlemas. Ever since the Middle Ages, they have been sold at fairs and they can be found in all flavors: apple, cheese, almond, elder or acacia blossom, or else deliciously simple, as in this old recipe. Nowadays they are known as *Pets-de-nonne*.

> Put some water in a saucepan with a walnut of butter and a little salt, and some finely chopped preserved citrus peel; boil these together on the stove; and having added two good handfuls of flour, stir it with all your strength until it comes away from the sides of the saucepan; then draw it aside and add two egg yolks which you mix well in, and continue in the same way, adding two egg yolks at a time, until ten or twelve have been added, so that your pastry is light; then spread some flour on a clean surface or table, flour your hands and stretch your pastry, one part at a time, all over. When it has rested, roll it out and cut it into small pieces, making sure that they do not stick to one another; and when you are ready to serve them, fry your fritters in the skillet in very hot butter or fresh pork fat; once cooked and nicely brown, take them out, sprinkle them with sugar and a little orange-flower water, and serve them very hot.

1 teaspoon salt
2 teaspoons sugar
⅓ cup (3½ oz/100 g) butter
1½ cups (5 oz/155 g) sifted all-purpose (plain) flour
5 eggs
1 qt (1 l) peanut (groundnut) oil
⅓ cup (3½ oz/100 g) sugar

Pour 2 cups (16 fl oz/500 ml) water into a heavy saucepan and add the salt, sugar and butter. Set over gentle heat and bring just to a boil. Remove from the heat at the first boil. Off the heat, sprinkle on the flour, stirring it in with a spatula. Return the saucepan to gentle heat and stir for about 1 minute, to dry the dough. Remove from the heat. Add the eggs, one by one, completely blending in each egg before adding the next one. Do not overwork the dough after the last egg — the puffs will be smooth and even.

When the dough is ready, heat the oil in a deep-fryer. When hot (about 350°F/180°C), spoon a small amount of the dough into the hot oil, pushing it with your fingers; it will fall in the shape of a small ball that will swell, brown and turn itself over in the hot oil, cooking in about 3 minutes.

When the fritters are cooked, remove with a skimmer and drain on paper towels.

Serve the fritters hot, arranged in a pyramid shape on a dish and sprinkle with sugar.

CRÈME BRÛLÉE

Crème brûlée   Serves 4

Literally "burnt custard," *crème brûlée* owes its name to the fact that sugar is caramelized over its surface, either under a broiler or, in bygone days, with a red-hot baker's shovel — but it is never burnt (*brûlée*). The contrast between the crunchy caramel topping and the thick smooth custard beneath is most delicious. Recipes such as this are to be found in all cookbooks from the eighteenth century onwards.

1 ¼ cups (10 fl oz/315 ml) milk
⅓ cup (3 fl oz/90 ml) heavy (double) cream
2 eggs
4 egg yolks
2 fl oz (60 ml) acacia honey
2 vanilla beans
3 tablespoons (1 ½ oz/45 g) packed brown sugar

Flowers and fruit, Jean Baptiste Monnoyer (1636–99); MUSEE DES BEAUX-ARTS, ORLEANS

Preheat the oven to 225°F (110°C/Gas ¼).

Pour the milk into a small saucepan and bring to a boil. Add the cream, mix for 30 seconds and remove from heat.

Break the eggs into a bowl; add the yolks and whisk. Add the honey and continue to whisk until the mixture whitens, but does not foam. Pour in the milk–cream mixture and whisk continuously.

Strain the mixture through a sieve. Divide among four ½ cup molds or other ovenproof dishes. Bake for 30 minutes with the 4 molds standing in a tray of water. Turn off the oven heat and let the custards stand for 15 minutes in the turned-off oven; the liquid center will set.

When the custards are cooked, remove them from the oven and set aside to cool. Cover and refrigerate for 2 to 8 hours.

When the custards are chilled, preheat the broiler (grill).

Meanwhile, slit the vanilla beans lengthwise. Remove the little black seeds with a pointed knife. Put them in a bowl and mix in the brown sugar. Sprinkle the scented sugar over the custards. Broil, close to the heat, for about 1½ minutes, until the sugar caramelizes. Set aside to cool. Refrigerate until serving time, but for no more than 2 hours, otherwise the humidity may cause the caramel to melt.

BLANCMANGE WITH WILD STRAWBERRIES

Blanc-manger aux fraises des bois   Serves 4

Blancmange goes back a long way. During the Middle Ages, this dish was known all over Europe, but the recipes were different in every country, their only common feature being the pursuit of the white color (although in the fifteenth century there were also *blanc-mangiers partys* [part], which, as the name suggests, were two-colored). The English made it with rice, the white part of the chicken (breast) and almond milk, while the French made it with chicken breast, broth and almonds. The contemporary version is a clingy cream made with gelatin and flavored with almond.

2 cups (16 fl oz/500 ml) milk
1 ¾ tablespoons (25 g) powdered (10 leaves) unflavored gelatin
¾ cup (6 oz/180 g) superfine (caster) sugar
½ teaspoon natural bitter almond extract (essence)
1 ¼ lb (600 g) wild strawberries

Crème brûlée (left); Blancmange with wild strawberries (right)

Pour ⅓ cup (3 fl oz/90 ml) of the milk into a saucepan and bring to a boil. Sprinkle on the gelatin and stir until dissolved. Remove from the heat and add the remaining milk, half the sugar and the bitter almond extract. Mix and set aside to cool.

Moisten four ½ cup molds. Divide 10 oz (315 g) of the wild strawberries among them. Pour on almond milk to cover. Cover and refrigerate for 4 to 6 hours.

Prepare the wild strawberry sauce. Push the

remaining 10 oz (315 g) fruit through the medium disk of a food mill into a nonreactive small saucepan. Add the remaining sugar and lemon juice. Bring to a boil and boil for 5 minutes. Remove from the heat and set aside to cool. Refrigerate until serving time.

To serve, immerse the bottoms of the molds in hot water. Invert onto 4 dishes. Garnish each blancmange with sauce, garnish with strawberries and serve.

WHITE CHEESECAKE

Gâteau au fromage blanc Serves 6

In the first French cookbooks, such as Taillevent's *Le Viandier* or the recipes from *Le Ménagier de Paris*, which both date from the fourteenth century, one can find tarts or cakes made with fresh cheese. This tradition has continued, often in rural areas.

*8 oz (250 g) fresh cheese, such as ricotta, cream
    cheese or Saint-Florentin, at room temperature*
1 teaspoon vanilla extract (essence)
½ cup (4 fl oz/125 ml) crème fraîche
⅔ cup (5 oz/155 g) superfine (caster) sugar
2 tablespoons all-purpose (plain) flour
4 eggs
1 grated zest (rind) of lemon

Preheat the oven to 350°F (180°C/Gas 4). Butter a 1¼ qt (1.25 l) soufflé dish. Sprinkle with sugar, turning the dish to coat with a thin layer of sugar all over the dish.

Place the cheese in the bowl of a food processor. Add the vanilla extract and *crème fraîche* and blend for 30 seconds. Add the superfine sugar, flour, eggs and lemon zest. Blend for

30 seconds. Pour the mixture into the soufflé dish.

Bake for 1 hour and 10 minutes, until the cake rises above the edge of the dish and is very golden. Remove from the oven; it will deflate slightly.

Turn the cake upside down on a plate and let stand for 30 minutes without removing the soufflé dish. Remove the soufflé dish and invert the cake onto a serving dish; its surface will be perfectly smooth and shiny. Refrigerate the cake for 12 hours before serving. Garnish the top of the cake with berries and leaves. Sprinkle caster sugar over the berries.

HONEY ICE-CREAM

Glace au miel Serves 4–5

During the turmoil of the Renaissance years, the French learned from the Italians the art of making ice-cream. Fruit-based sherbets were particularly appreciated and became popular in Parisian cafés after the opening in the seventeenth century of the Café Procope, named after its owner, which specialized in ice-creams and sherbets. Until the end of the nineteenth century, there was in Paris, in Rue Glacière, a large underground warehouse

White cheese cake (left); Honey ice-cream (right)

where natural ice brought from high mountains in winter was conserved and supplied to vendors of ice-cream or to rich Parisians living on a grand scale.

1 ⅓ cups (11 fl oz/345 ml) milk
2 egg yolks
¼ cup (1 ¾ oz/50 g) superfine (caster) sugar
¼ cup plus 1 tablespoon (2 ½ fl oz/75 ml) crème fraîche
3 ½ fl oz (100 ml) strong-flavored honey, such as lavender, mille-fleurs, foret or rosemary

Bring the milk to a boil in a small saucepan. In another saucepan, whisk the egg yolks with the sugar. Add the milk in a thin stream, whisking constantly. Put the pot over low heat. Cook as for a custard, stirring constantly and without letting it boil, until the mixture coats a spoon, 5 to 6 minutes. Remove the pot from the heat and set aside to cool.

Strain the cooled custard into the bowl of a mixer. Add the *crème fraîche* and honey and mix at high speed for about 2 minutes, until thick and frothy.

Pour the mixture into an ice-cream maker and freeze according to the manufacturer's instructions.

To serve, scoop the ice-cream into cups or dishes. Drizzle ice-cream with extra honey. Serve with almond biscuits and a mixture of red fruits: wild strawberries, raspberries or redcurrants garnished with lavender.

CHESTNUT BAVARIAN CREAM

Bavarois aux marrons   Serves 6

Originally, in the seventeenth and eighteenth centuries, a *bavarois* was a drink made with flavored milk, thickened by adding a little fern. As time went on, it became a pastry cream, solidified with gelatin, and flavored with all sorts of scents.

1 lb (500 g) fresh chestnuts
1 vanilla bean, split lengthwise
2 cups (16 fl oz/500 ml) milk
1 cup (8 fl oz/250 ml) heavy (double) cream
⅓ cup (3 oz/90 g) superfine (caster) sugar
1 teaspoon (5 g) powdered (2 leaves) unflavored gelatin
1 tablespoon dark rum

Chestnut bavarian cream

1 ½ oz (50 g) bittersweet chocolate, grated into curls
unsweetened cocoa powder

Slit the chestnut shells and immerse in boiling water. Cook for 5 minutes; drain and cool under running water. Remove the shell and the thin brown skin that covers the chestnuts.

Place the chestnuts in a saucepan. Add the vanilla bean and milk. Bring to a boil, reduce the heat and simmer, stirring often, for 1 hour, until the milk has almost completely evaporated and the chestnuts have broken down. Discard the vanilla bean.

Heat 3 tablespoons of the cream in a small pan with half the sugar. Bring to a boil. Sprinkle on the gelatin and stir to dissolve. Remove from the heat.

Pour the chestnuts into the bowl of a food processor and blend to a very fine purée. Add the rum and the gelatin–cream mixture and process again. Pour the purée into a large bowl.

Beat the remaining cream with the remaining sugar until it forms peaks. Gently mix the whipped cream into the chestnut purée. Fold in the chocolate curls. Divide the mixture among 6 small ramekins or spoon into a large ribbed mold. Cover and refrigerate for 8 hours.

Just before serving, immerse the bottoms of the molds in hot water. Unmold the mousses onto serving plates. Sift the cocoa over the tops.

CARAMELIZED BANANA CHARLOTTE

Charlotte aux bananes caramélisées   Serves 6

A charlotte is a preparation set with gelatin or cream, or a thick purée, contained in a mold lined with biscuits, slices of bread or brioche (sweet bread). In this recipe, the biscuits are replaced by slightly green bananas. Charlottes made a good impression on middle-class dessert menus of the nineteenth century. With the passing years, the preparations became lighter, and the sauces with which they were served became more sophisticated.

5 ripe bananas
¼ cup (2 oz/60 g) butter
1 cup (8 oz/250 g) superfine (caster) sugar
1 teaspoon (5 g) powdered (2 leaves) unflavored gelatin
3 tablespoons dark rum
grated zest (rind) of 1 lemon
1⅓ cups (10 fl oz/315 ml) heavy (double) cream
2 eggwhites
4 slightly green bananas

Peel 3 of the ripe bananas, slice them and set aside 10 oz (300 g).

Melt 1½ tablespoons (¾ oz/20 g) butter in a 10¼ inch (26 cm) nonstick skillet over medium heat. Add ¼ cup (1½ oz/45 g) of the sugar and the banana slices. Brown the bananas for about 5 minutes. Pour the contents of the skillet into the bowl of a food processor. Add the gelatin and process to a fine purée. Add 2 tablespoons of the rum and the lemon zest. Pour the mixture into a bowl and set aside to cool.

Whip ⅔ cup (5 fl oz/155 ml) of the cream and 1 tablespoon of the sugar until stiff. Fold into the banana purée.

Champagne, Gaston Latouche (1854–1913);
MUSEE DES BEAUX-ARTS, ROUEN

246

Beat the eggwhites with 1 tablespoon of sugar until smooth and shiny. Gently fold into the banana purée.

Peel the green bananas and cut them diagonally into ¼ inch (5 mm) thick slices, 1½ inches (4 cm) long. Melt the remaining 2½ tablespoons butter in a saucepan. Add 3 tablespoons of sugar. Add the green banana slices and cook until caramelized on both sides.

Line the bottom of a 1½ qt (1.5 l) charlotte mold with the green banana slices. Add the banana purée and smooth the surface. Cover with plastic and freeze the charlotte for 2 hours. Then refrigerate for 1 hour.

During this time, prepare the sauce. Combine the remaining 7 tablespoons of sugar and 3 tablespoons of water in a saucepan. Bring to a boil and cook until the caramel is golden. Stop the cooking by immersing the bottom of the pot in cold water. Set aside.

Peel the remaining 2 ripe bananas. In a blender or processor, blend the bananas with the remaining ⅔ cup (5 fl oz/155 ml) of cream. Pour the purée into the caramel and return the pot to gentle heat. Cook, stirring, for 5 minutes. Stir in the remaining 1 tablespoon of rum.

When about to serve, immerse the charlotte mold for 30 seconds in hot water. Unmold the charlotte onto a serving platter. Warm the sauce and serve it separately, in a sauceboat.

ICED NOUGAT

Nougat glacé   Serves 6

N ougat is a traditional delicacy from the South of France and, more particularly, from the city of Montélimar. Its original recipe is a delicate mixture of honey, almonds, candied fruits and eggwhites. This iced nougat uses the basic ingredients of the traditional recipe and turns them into a light cream, which, once frozen, can be sliced like a cake.

2½ oz (75 g) blanched pistachios
½ cup (4 oz/125 g) superfine (caster) sugar
5 oz (155 g) blanched almonds
3½ fl oz (100 ml) acacia honey
3 eggs, separated
2 tablespoons orange-flower water
1½ cups (13 fl oz/410 ml) chilled heavy (double) cream
5 oz (155 g) candied (crystallized) cherries, diced

Caramelized banana charlotte (top); Iced nougat (bottom)

Brown the pistachios in a nonstick skillet. Sprinkle with 1 teaspoon of the sugar and stir until lightly caramelized. Let them cool on a dish. Wash and dry the skillet.

Lightly brown the almonds in the skillet. Sprinkle with 1 tablespoon of sugar and stir until lightly caramelized. Cool on a dish.

Gently heat the honey in a small saucepan for 3 minutes. Beat the eggwhites until stiff. Add the boiling honey in a thin stream, beating constantly until the whites are smooth, shiny and cold. Beat in the orange-flower water.

Add the remaining sugar to the egg yolks and beat until the mixture lightens in color. Fold in the eggwhites.

Whip the cream until it forms peaks. Fold into the nougat mixture.

Coarsely crush the almonds and pistachios with a pestle. Add to the nougat mixture with the cherries.

Line a cake dish 11 x 4 inches (28 x 10 cm) long with plastic wrap. Pour in the nougat mixture and smooth the top. Cover with plastic and freeze for 12 hours.

At the end of that time, remove from the freezer and refrigerate for up to 4 hours until serving time.

Just before serving, unmold onto a serving platter and remove the adhesive sheet. Serve the iced nougat in slices.

This nougat can be served with a mixed red fruit sauce made with 1 lb (500 g) of fruit mixed with ⅓ cup (3 fl oz/90 ml) of sugar cane syrup and 3 tablespoons of lemon juice.

Chocolate truffles (bottom); Almond tuiles (top)

CHOCOLATE TRUFFLES

Truffes au chocolat   Makes about 30 truffles

Great lovers of this dish say it is the ultimate combination of sweet and bitter tastes. This most French of confectioneries, whose name reminds one of the famous *diamant noir* (black diamond) of cuisine, is extensively consumed around Christmas and New Years.

1 fl oz (30 ml) orange tree honey
⅓ cup (3½ fl oz/100 ml) crème fraîche
grated zest (rind) of 1 lemon

6½ oz (200 g) bittersweet chocolate, coarsely chopped
2 tablespoons (1 oz/30 g) butter, softened
unsweetened cocoa powder

In a nonreactive saucepan, combine the honey, *crème fraîche* and lemon zest. Bring to a boil, cover and set aside for 15 minutes.

Meanwhile, melt the chocolate in a double-boiler or in the microwave oven. Add the butter and stir until melted.

Strain the honey mixture into the chocolate. Stir and cool. Then use a whisk to aerate the mixture. Cover and refrigerate for about 30 minutes, until set.

Sift the cocoa into a deep plate. Remove the mixture from the refrigerator and work it with a spatula so as to make it flexible. Take a dab of the truffle mixture and roll it in the cocoa. Continue until all of the mixture is used.

Arrange the truffles in individual paper cups and store airtight. Refrigerate for 12 hours before serving.

ALMOND TUILES

Tuiles aux amandes   Serves 6

Across between biscuits, confectionery and dessert, these cookies can be served with creams, ice-cream or mousses. Their exquisite taste is based on the very old combination of almonds and sugar, which originated around the Mediterranean but from there spread throughout Europe.

2 tablespoons all-purpose (plain) flour
⅓ cup (3 oz/90 g) superfine (caster) sugar
4 oz (125 g) slivered (flaked) almonds
2 eggwhites
2 tablespoons (1 oz/30 g) melted butter

Combine the flour, sugar and almonds in a bowl. Add the eggwhites and butter and mix well. Cover the bowl and refrigerate for 12 hours.

At the end of this time, preheat the oven to 325°F (170°C/Gas 3). Lightly butter 2 large nonstick baking sheets. With this quantity of dough you can make 12 medium-size tuiles or 6 large ones. Depending on your choice, spoon very thin circles of the batter over the baking sheets. The batter should be spread *very* thin — use the back of a spoon.

Slide one sheet into the oven and bake 7 to 8 minutes; watch the cooking — they must be golden. Remove from the oven and immediately lift off the baking sheets with a slotted spatula; they will be soft and pliable. Arrange over the curve of a rolling pin if they are small, or over a bottle if they are larger. Very quickly they will dry into a beautiful curved shape. Cool on a rack. Meanwhile, cook the other tuiles the same way.

Eat the tuiles soon after they are cooked. You may add fine strips of pistachios, candied orange peels or tiny chocolate flakes.

ICED GRAND MARNIER MOUSSE

Mousse glacée au Grand Marnier   Serves 6

Light and airy mousses were somewhat rejected during the nineteenth century as middle-class values of stability and certainty were favored. The subtle and delicate preparations of the preceding centuries were forgotten and it was left to the great turning point of Nouvelle Cuisine, in the 1970s, to unveil a whole range of new such creations that were light and frothy, either savory or sweet. The following recipe is a delicious example of this revival.

10 oz (315 g) kumquats
1 cup (8 oz/250 g) superfine (caster) sugar
3 drops lemon juice
3.75 g powdered (1½ leaves) unflavored gelatin
6 eggs
⅓ cup (3 fl oz/90 ml) Grand Marnier liqueur
12 fl oz (350 ml) fresh orange juice
1⅓ cups (11 fl oz/45 ml) crème fraîche
4 fl oz (125 ml) honey

Prepare the kumquats 24 hours ahead. Cut each kumquat into slices and remove the seeds. Combine the kumquats and ½ cup (4 oz/125 g) of the sugar in a bowl. Set aside for 24 hours.

Prepare the mousse 12 hours ahead. Combine the remaining ½ cup (4 oz/125 g) sugar and the lemon juice in a nonreactive saucepan. Add 3 tablespoons of water and bring to a boil. Simmer for 1 minute. Sprinkle on the gelatin and stir until dissolved. Set aside to cool.

Beat the eggs in a large bowl. Slowly pour the syrup into the eggs and whisk constantly until the mixture is cold. Add the Grand Marnier and the *crème fraîche* and whisk again.

Iced Grand Marnier mousse

Butter a 6¼ inch (16 cm) soufflé dish. Pour in the mixture. Cover and freeze for 12 hours.

Prepare the sauce. Combine the orange juice and honey in a saucepan and bring to a boil. Keep boiling until reduced to about ¾ cup (6 fl oz/185 ml) of syrupy sauce. Keep in a cool place.

One hour before serving, remove the mousse from the freezer and refrigerate.

When about to serve, immerse the bottom of the soufflé dish in hot water for a few seconds. Unmold onto a dish. Arrange the kumquats on top of mousse and pour on the sauce.

CHOCOLATE TART

Tarte au chocolat   Serves 6–8

O riginally, tarts were savory as well as sweet. Both kinds are found in *Le Ménagier de Paris* (1393) and in Taillevent's *Viandier* (*c*.1370). But for chocolate lovers, this contemporary version is simply irresistible.

2 cups (8 oz/250 g) white flour

½ cup (4 oz/125 g) butter, softened

1 tablespoon superfine (caster) sugar

1 pinch salt

⅔ cup (6 fl oz/185 ml) milk

1¾ cups (13 fl oz/410 ml) heavy (double) cream

13 oz (410 g) bittersweet chocolate, coarsely chopped

8 eggs

Prepare the pastry. Sift the flour, sugar and salt into the bowl of a food processor and add chopped butter. Process until mixture resembles fine breadcrumbs. Gradually add ¼ cup (2 fl oz/ 60 ml) water and process until the mixture comes together to form a ball. Pat the dough into a disk, wrap in plastic and refrigerate for 3 hours.

Preheat the oven to 450°F (230°C/Gas 8). Butter a 9 inch (23 cm) tart pan.

Roll out the pastry into a thin circle. Fit the dough into the mold. Cover with waxed paper and pie weights or dried beans. Bake the shell for 20 minutes.

During this time, prepare the filling. Combine the milk and cream in a saucepan and bring to a boil. Add the chocolate and remove from the heat. Set aside for 10 minutes, until the chocolate melts. Whisk until smooth. Whisk in the eggs.

Remove the weights from the tart shell. Strain the chocolate mixture through a sieve into the shell.

Reduce the oven to 375°F (190°C/Gas 5). Bake the tart for 35 minutes. Remove to a rack to cool. Unmold and serve warm or cold, dusted with cocoa and garnished with chocolate curls.

The lunch of bitter chocolate, Juan de Zurbaràn (1620–49); MUSEE DES BEAUX-ARTS BESANCON

Chocolate tart

BIBLIOGRAPHY

Aaron, J. P. *Le mangeur du XIXème siècle* (available in English as *The Art of Eating in France: Manners and Menus in the Nineteenth Century)* Paris: Robert Laffont, 1973

Belon, Pierre *L'histoire naturelle des oiseaux avec leurs descriptions et naïfs portraicts retirez du naturel (The Natural History of Birds, with Descriptions and Simple Illustrations from Nature)* 7 volumes, Paris: 1555

Bernier, B. *Antonin Carême* Paris: Grasset, 1989

Braudel, F. "Alimentation et catégories de l'histoire" ("Diet and Schools of History") in J. J. Hermandiquer, *Pour une histoire de l'alimentation (Towards a History of Diet)* Paris: Armand Colin, 1970, pp. 15–19

Brillat-Savarin *La physiologie du goût, avec une lecture de Roland Barthes* (available in English as *The Philosopher in the Kitchen*, translated by Anne Drayton London: Penguin) Paris: Hermann, 1975

Capatti, A. *Le goût du nouveau: origines de la modernité alimentaire (The Taste for Novelty: Origins of Alimentary Modernity)* Paris: Albin Michel, 1990

Carême, Antonin "Aphorismes, pensées et maximes" ("Aphorisms, Thoughts and Maxims") in *Les classiques de la table à l'usage des praticiens et des gens du monde (The Classics of the Table, Written for Practitioners and Gentlemen)*, edited by Alfred Charles and Frederic Fayot, Paris: 1843

Civilisation matérielle, économie et capitalisme, XVe–XVIIIe siècles (available in English as *Civilisation and Capitalism, Fifteenth to Eighteenth Century* London: Weidenfeld & Nicolson, 1973) 3 volumes, Paris: Armand Colin, 1979

de Bonnefons, Nicholas *Les délices de la campagne. Suite du jardinier françois où est enseigné à préparer pour l'usage de la vie tout ce qui croist sur la terre et dans les eaux, dédié aux dames mesnagères (The Joys of Country Living. Sequel to the French Gardener, Wherein are Taught Manners of Preparation of Everything That Grows in Earth or in the Water, for the Sustenance of the Body, Dedicated to the Lady of the House)* Paris: 1654, 1679 and 1682

"La distinction par le goût" ("Taste as a Means of Social Distinction") in *Histoire de la vie privée de la Renaissance au Siècle des Lumières (History of Domestic Life, from the Renaissance to the Enlightenment)* Paris: Le Seuil, 1986 pp. 265–309

Dubois, Urbain *La cuisine classique (Classical Cuisine)* Paris: 1876

Duby, G. *Guerriers et paysans (Warriors and Peasants)* Paris: Gallimard, 1973

Flandrin, J.-L. "Gastronomie historique: l'ancien service à la française" (Historical Gastronomy: The Former French Manner of Serving Meals") *L'Histoire* 20, 1980, pp. 90–2

Ketcham-Wheaton, Barbara *L'office et la bouche, histoire des moeurs de la table en France* (first published in English as *Savouring the Past: The French Kitchen and Table from 1300 to 1789* London: Chatto & Windus, 1983) Paris: Calmann Levy, 1984

La Chapelle Vincent *Le cuisinier moderne qui apprend à donner à manger toutes sortes de repas en gras et en maigre, d'une manière plus délicate que ce qui a été écrit jusqu'à présent (The Modern Cook, Which Instructs How to Prepare and Serve All Kinds of Meals for Both Meat-eating and Fish-eating Days in a More Refined Style Than That Which Has Been Written Until Now)* 4 volumes, La Haye: 1735

Laurioux, Bruno "Le mangeur de l'an mil" ("Dining in the Year 1000") *L'Histoire* 73, 1984

————— *Le Moyen Age à table (Eating in Medieval Times)* Paris: 1989

La Varenne *Le cuisinier François (The French Cook)*, edited by J.-L. Flandrin, J. P. Hyman and M. Hyman, Paris: Montalba, 1983

LSR *L'art de bien traiter, divisé en trois parties. Ouvrage nouveau, curieux et fort galant utile à toutes personnes et conditions (The Art of Proper Catering, Divided into Three Parts. A New Work, Original and Well-mannered, Useful to Persons in All Walks of Life)* Paris: 1674

Marin, François *Les dons de Comus ou les delices de la table (The Gifts of Comus or the Pleasures of the Table)* Paris:1739

Massialot, François *Le nouveau cuisinier royal et bourgeois (The New Cook, Royal and Bourgeois)* 3 volumes, Paris: 1748

Le ménagier de Paris, traité de morale et d'economie domestique, par un bourgeois Parisien, composé vers 1393 (available in English as *The Goodman of Paris: A Treatise on Moral and Domestic Economy by a Citizen of Paris*, translated by Eileen Power, London: Routledge, 1928) Paris: Jerôme Pichon, 1848, revised in 2 volumes, Geneva: Slatkine Reprints

Menon *La cuisine bourgeoise (Bourgeois Cooking)* New edition, Paris: 1807

Moulin, L. *Les liturgies de la table (The Ceremonies of Dining)* Paris: Albin Michel, 1989

Neirinck, E. and Poulain, J. P. *Histoire de la cuisine et des cuisiniers, techniques culinaires et pratiques de table en France du Moyen Age à nos jours (History of Cooking and of Cooks, Culinary Techniques and Eating Habits in France from the Medieval Period to the Present Day)* Paris: Jacques Lanore, 1988

La nouvelle maison rustique ou économi générale de tous les biens de campagne (The New Country House Manual, or Complete Household Guide for Country-dwellers) 5th edition, Paris: 1740

"Plaisirs et angoisses de la fourchette" ("Pleasures and Tortures of the Fork") *Autrement* 108, September 1989

Revel, J.-F. *La sensibilité gastronomique de l'antiquité à nos jours. Un festin de paroles* (available in English as *Culture and Cuisine: A Journey through the History of Food)* Paris: Suger, 1985

Rival, N. *Grimod de la Reynière, le gourmand gentilhomme (Grimod de la Reynière: The Gentleman Gourmand)* Paris: Le Pré aux Clercs, 1983

"Les sauces légères du Moyen Age" ("Medieval Light Sauces") *L'Histoire* 35, pp. 87–9

Stouff, Louis *Ravitaillement et alimentation en Provence aux XIVe et XVe siècles (Food Supply and Diet in Provence in the Fourteenth and Fifteenth Centuries)* Paris La Haye: Mouton, 1970

Taillevent, Guillaume Tirel *Le viandier (The Cook's Notebook)* Jerôme Pichon and Georges Vicaire: 1892, revised and enlarged by S. Martinet, Geneva: Slatkine, 1967

INDEX

ACKNOWLEDGMENTS

HISTORICAL PICTURES

Weldon Russell Pty Ltd would like to thank the following photographic libraries and galleries for supplying pictures for reproduction from their collections:

G. Dagli Orti: pp. 12 (top and bottom), 15, 17, 18, 19, 20, 22, 24, 26, 27, 29, 33, 34–35, 45, 48, 52, 54, 68, 76, 78, 98, 100, 101, 109, 112, 124, 126 (top), 128, 129, 138, 144, 146–47, 151, 152, 160, 165, 173, 174, 180, 181, 182, 184, 185, 188, 194, 198, 207 (top), 209, 218, 224, 226 (bottom) 246, 250.

Musee Royaux des Beaux-Arts de Belgique: pp. 74–75.

Photographie Giraudon: Bridgeman-Giraudon: pp. 3, 28, 38, 81, 170, 204, 242. BL-Giraudon: pp. 88, 105. Flammarion-Giraudon: pp. 155. Giraudon: front cover, back cover, endpapers, pp. 6, 8–9, 13, 21, 23, 25, 32, 39 (bottom), 46–47, 61, 79 (bottom), 85, 92, 96–97, 104, 122–23, 148, 154, 176–77, 178, 183, 191, 206, 207 (bottom), 208 (top and bottom), 221, 222–23, 227, 228, 230, 238. Lauros-Giraudon: pp. 2, 4–5, 14, 16, 29 (top), 30, 31, 39 (top), 42, 50, 51, 53, 56, 64, 70, 73, 79 (top), 80, 83, 102, 103, 119, 126 (bottom), 127, 133, 134, 137, 141, 142, 150, 153, 169, 197, 201, 202–203, 210, 226 (top), 229, 235.

Scala: pp. 10, 36.

Copyright information: Louise Abbema © SPADEM; Laurent Adenot: rights reserved; Pierre Bonnard © ADAGP/SPADEM; Georges Braque © ADAGP/SPADEM; Victor Gilbert: rights reserved; Jules Grün © SPADEM; Henri Lerolle: rights reserved; Henri Lesidaner: rights reserved; Edouard Pignon © SPADEM; Georges Rohner © ADAGP; Charles Roussel: rights reserved; Louis Valtat © ADAGP; Edouard Vuillard © SPADEM.

FOOD PHOTOGRAPHY

Jon Bader (photographer) and Marie Hélène Clauzon (home economist and food stylist): pp. 41, 44, 55, 58, 60, 63, 66, 67, 68, 71, 83, 84, 86, 87, 91, 94, 108, 110, 114, 117, 120, 131, 143, 145, 159, 168.

Jon Bader (photographer) and Carolyn Fienberg (home economist and food stylist), assisted by Jo Forrest: pp. 156, 161, 162, 164, 175, 187, 189, 192, 193, 195, 200, 211, 214, 215, 217, 219, 234, 237, 240, 243, 244, 245, 248, 249, 251.

Rowan Fotheringham (photographer) and Marie Hélène Clauzon (home economist and food stylist): pp. 106, 107, 158, 166, 171, 172, 186, 188, 190, 196, 197, 199, 212, 213, 216, 220, 231, 232, 233, 236, 239, 241, 247.

Rowan Fotheringham (photographer) and Carolyn Fienberg (home economist and food stylist), assisted by Jo Forrest: pp. 40, 43, 57, 59, 62, 65, 69, 72, 82, 89, 90, 93, 95, 111, 113, 115, 116, 118, 121, 132, 135, 136, 139, 140, 163, 167.

Weldon Russell would like to thank the following companies who lent props for the food photography: Country Floors; glassware from Bohemia Crystal; Les Olivades; Limoges; Mikasa Tableware; Noritake; Old Country Furniture, Balmain; silver from Oneida; fabric from I. Redelman and Son; Rivtex; Robertson & Meads; Royal Doulton; Villeroy & Bosch; Wedgwood.

OVEN TEMPERATURE CONVERSIONS

° Celsius	° Fahrenheit	Gas Mark
110°C	225°F	¼
130	250	½
140	275	1
150	300	2
170	325	3
180	350	4
190	375	5
200	400	6
220	425	7
230	450	8
240	475	9